CHOOSING A SCHOOL

Second-Level Education in Ireland

CHOOSING A SCHOOL

Second-Level Education in Ireland

Deirdre Raftery & Catherine KilBride

MERCIER PRESS
WHAT YOU NEED TO READ

Mercier Press
Douglas Village, Cork
www.mercierpress.ie

Trade enquiries to Columba Mercier Distribution,
55a Spruce Avenue, Stillorgan Industrial Park, Blackrock, Dublin

© Deirdre Raftery and Catherine KilBride, 2007
ISBN: 978 1 85635 530 8

10 9 8 7 6 5 4 3 2 1

Mercier Press receives financial assistance from
the Arts Council/An Chomhairle Ealaíon

Printed and bound in Ireland by Colour Books Ltd.

**This book
is dedicated with affection
to our friends and our former students
in the teaching profession.**

Contents

Figures and Tables

List of Figures

List of Tables

Acknowledgements

The authors gratefully acknowledge the following: the parents who co-operated with this research; the administrative and teaching staff at second-level schools throughout Ireland who were most helpful; the school principals who welcomed us into their schools, gave generously of their time and facilitated interviews; the School of Education and Lifelong Learning, College of Human Sciences, UCD; the Department of Education and Science; the State Examinations Commission; the National Council for Curriculum and Assessment; Cambridge University Library; University College Dublin Library; and the editorial staff of Mercier Press. Our deepest gratitude is reserved for our friends and families for their continued interest and support, particularly Melissa KilBride.

Introduction

Who is this book for?

If you've picked up this book, you are probably thinking about how you will choose the right second-level school for your child.

Your child may be in primary school and you have important decisions to make that will impact on his happiness and well-being until he is a young adult. You are not alone in this. The parents of your child's friends are also facing this decision. They are exchanging views at the school gate; they are asking questions whenever you meet them. Indeed, many report that this has become the main topic of conversation among parents of children in this age group. But what you hear may be confusing you rather than helping you. You gather prospectuses from local schools, but they all seem to be saying the same thing. You read media reports about 'good' schools, yet these reports don't help you to decide whether these schools will be 'good' for *your* child.

Or maybe you are further along in the process and you have short-listed a handful of schools. These might include one close to home; one with a 'good reputation'; and one where some of your child's friends say they are going. You have completed application forms for all three and, in some cases, you may have paid an application fee. You are still not sure which school will be the best for *your* child and the time has come to make a final decision.

You may live in an area where one school is the obvious choice. Typically, the pupils from your child's primary school go on to that school. You are very happy with the reputation of the school. However, you want to make sure you have all the relevant information that indicates it will suit *your* child.

The challenges facing you may be greater if you have recently moved – or moved back – to this country. You need to become familiar with the complexities of a different system, including the different school types, the programmes and examination systems, the application process and, indeed, the costs involved in education in this country.

Your child may already be in a second-level school and you're thinking of making a change. This may be because your child is unhappy and unsettled and you need to make a confident decision about moving him. Or maybe you have one child who is doing well in a particular school, but you are not convinced that this will be the right school for a younger sibling. You may even be quite content with the second-level school that your child is attending, but you have become aware that other parents are moving their children out of that school and as a result you are beginning to doubt your own decision.

Why is school choice important?

On one hand you may feel that your concerns are legitimate but, on the other, you may feel foolish articulating them. You are not being foolish. Your concern for your child's welfare is always legitimate. Second only to home/family, school plays the most significant formative role in your child's life. The school is not only a place where your child will enjoy academic and sporting activities. School is also the place where friendships are made, values are learned and pupils experience both success and failure. Over the six years of second-level education, your child will grow from being highly dependent on your guidance to becoming an independent learner and more mature human being. For this reason, selecting the right school for your child is of great importance. Schools are simply not 'one-size-fits-all'. Even within the same school, different pupils will experience the school in a different way.

How will this book help you?

You want the best for your child. You want your child to feel confident and happy. You want her to be educated in an atmosphere that is both secure and disciplined and you want her to feel motivated and enthusiastic about learning. The most suitable school for your child is the one that provides the environment in which her potential will be realised. This book will help you to make informed decisions in the search for the right school for your child.

How should you use this book?

The underlying principle of this book is that you know your child best. You are responsible for making all the important decisions to do with his schooling. But you need to inform yourself about the education system so that you can use this knowledge when choosing a school.

For simplicity, we have assumed that the reader has no prior knowledge of the second-level education system in Ireland, so we attempt to give a clear overview of this area. However, chapters are written in a stand-alone style, so that you may dip in and out of the book. For example, chapter one has a lot of information on how the second-level system operates and Appendix A explains the curriculum and examinations process in more detail. If you have recent experience of the Irish education system, you may choose to skip those sections and focus instead on the sections dealing specifically with the issues involved in choosing a school. If you are considering boarding schools, you may find useful guidance in chapter five. If you are considering sending your sons and daughters to different schools, you may want to see what some research (summarised in chapter four) says about how pupils perform in single-sex and mixed schools. You may also be interested in hearing what parents and principals have to say about the importance of the happiness of the pupil (chapters five and six).

How is the book structured?

- **Chapter One** will help you to understand the education system. It includes an overview of how the system operates and how it evolved. It contains sections on the different school types, the structure of second-level education and the programmes offered. It also deals with issues related to getting a place for your child in a second-level school. These include how you make an application and how you enrol your child in a school; your rights; the cost of education; and the link between second-level schooling and eventual progression to third-level education, training and work.
- **Chapter Two** brings you some of the most important research and information on how school choice is made. You can examine what has emerged from other countries on issues such as matching the child to

the school and how parents use networking and the grapevine to gather information.

- **Chapter Three** addresses the question, 'What makes a good school good?' It draws on Irish research on academic results, subject choice, streaming/banding and school size. The chapter also looks at school discipline, teacher expectations and school management.

- **Chapter Four** gives you the opportunity to consider the differences between single-sex and mixed schools and to look at the relative merits of both. It draws on information about the examination performance of boys and girls in both single-sex and mixed schools. The chapter also comments on co-education and personal/social development.

- **Chapter Five** brings you the views of other parents involved in school choice. Among these are parents of one child; parents of several children whom they chose to send to different schools; parents who opted for boarding schools and parents who opted for *gaelscoileanna*. The issues discussed include whether the chosen school should be near home, whether different schools should be chosen for siblings and moving your child to a new school in the course of second-level education.

- **Chapter Six** introduces the voices of school principals. You can read their views on a range of questions such as: should your child be involved in the choice of school? They also discuss how a school develops a particular reputation. They express their concern for the happiness of their pupils in a disciplined environment.

- **Appendix A** sets out in detail the programmes and examinations prescribed by the National Council for Curriculum and Assessment. Here you can see, for example, the alternative courses available in the Junior Cycle and in the Senior Cycle, as well as the different examinations on offer.

- **Appendix B** provides you with the full listing of second-level schools, with details such as school type, the enrolment figures, whether they are single-sex or mixed, whether they are fee-paying, whether they are boarding schools and whether tuition is given entirely through the medium of Irish. The schools are ordered alphabetically by county and, in the case of Dublin, by post code.

Authors' comments

What we have tried to do is to create a volume that will be a useful, readable and above all helpful guide to anyone living in Ireland, whose children will soon be entering the second-level system. We have used the most recent data available at the time of writing. Throughout the volume we make frequent reference to 'parents'. We dispense with the use of the additional term 'guardians' for editorial reasons, although we recognise that many children are raised by persons other than their parents. We have made every attempt to use inclusive language. We have avoided using the composite 'he/she' by using both male and female personal pronouns. We also make sustained use of the terms, 'child' and 'children'. We do so because at point of entry to second-level education, pupils are usually twelve-year-old children. We accept that some of our readers will be using the book in order to make a decision about moving an older child to a new school and where appropriate we occasionally make use of the terms 'teenager' and 'pupil'. Other readers will be involved in education, either at pre-service or in-career stages and may be teaching teenage pupils. However, for simplicity, we most frequently use the term 'child'. We do so knowing that parents think affectionately of their offspring as children even when they have grown into adults and that teachers in school are always *in loco parentis*. Just how older children make the transition to adulthood, in an environment that is both stimulating and secure, is part of the concern of this book. We hope it supports both parents and educators and demonstrates the extraordinary care and commitment to the child that we found in second-level schools all over Ireland.

1 Understanding the Education System

This chapter opens with an overview of how the education system operates. It then outlines how the system evolved. Within this section, the different school types are explained: secondary, vocational, community and comprehensive. The chapter then describes for you how the education system is structured in Junior Cycle, Transition Year and Senior Cycle and summarises the different education programmes offered. Issues such as applications, enrolment and school fees are examined and the chapter concludes with a section on progression to third-level education, training and work.

How does the school system operate?

Schooling in Ireland takes place over two distinct stages: **primary schooling** (first level) and **post-primary schooling** (second level). Primary schooling ends when children reach sixth class – at about twelve years of age. Education is compulsory from age six to sixteen or until students have completed three years of second-level education. Some primary schools are attached to a secondary school and pupils automatically transfer to that school in the autumn after their primary education is completed. In that case, the primary school is a 'feeder school' to the affiliated secondary school, although in many instances children from other schools will also join the school for second-level education. In such schools it is not uncommon to have a single sixth class (of about thirty pupils) which joins with one or two new class groups to form the first-year cohort of the second-level school. Most primary schools do not have second-level schools attached. The national school system provides education at primary level only. Parents whose children have attended a national school will have to make a decision about where to send their child for second-level education. They are not the only parents facing such a decision – some parents whose children are in 'feeder' schools make a decision to move the child to a different school after primary education is complete. Those parents who decide that their child should progress to the affiliated second-level school are also making a choice.

How did the system evolve?

In order to understand how the education system now operates, we need to look at key stages in its development, which help to explain some of its unique features. For example, parents who have been educated outside Ireland may be struck by the fact that so many of our schools are single-sex schools. Our long tradition of single-sex secondary education is more easily understood when we look at another distinguishing feature of the Irish education system: the significant involvement of the Catholic religious orders in founding and managing schools and in teaching at every level. Parents who were educated within Ireland will be familiar with this history, but may be interested to know about innovations and changes in recent decades, such as multi-denominational and mixed schools.

Developments in the nineteenth century

Education in Ireland has been characterised by the involvement of both Church and State. The control of schooling has been a major feature of educational debate and the records of this debate date back to Penal times. In the late seventeenth and early eighteenth centuries, when Ireland was subject to British rule, a number of laws relating to education were passed that severely curtailed educational provision for the 'native' Catholic population and enforced harsh penalties if these laws were broken. These Penal Laws prohibited Catholics from establishing schools to teach Catholic children and also prevented them from sending their children overseas to be educated in Catholic countries. Schoolmasters who violated these laws could be imprisoned and deported. At this point, British government aid for education was channelled through Protestant voluntary societies who also operated schools for the poor. No Catholic schools received state support. The start of the nineteenth century saw the emergence of a consensus that there should be a state-funded 'mixed' education system, which would unite children from different churches and that state funding should not be channelled through the Protestant education societies. The Catholic population became more vocal in their demands for schooling and the repeal of relevant Penal Laws at the end of the eighteenth century meant that Catholic religious orders could establish themselves in teaching. Orders such as the Sisters of Mercy, Presentation Sisters and Christian Brothers grew significantly in the first half of the twentieth century and other orders, including the Jesuits, Dominicans, Ursulines, Vincentians and the Loreto Sisters, opened several schools.

Formal second-level examinations were introduced with the passing of the Intermediate Education (Ireland) Act of 1878. This act provided funding for annual public examinations and paid 'results' money to schools on the basis of the success of their pupils in the examinations. From the start, the Intermediate examination became the passport into well-paid clerical jobs for many successful candidates and it also became the route to university degrees which became increasingly available to the Catholic lay population (both men and women) after 1879.

Provision was made for technical education in the late nineteenth century and the Agriculture and Technical Instruction (Ireland) Act was passed in 1899. Under this legislation, the Department of Agriculture and Technical Instruction established a system of technical education. In due course, the vocational education system of the 1930s (see page 27) would develop from this late nineteenth century initiative.

Developments in the twentieth century: primary education

In December 1921, with the signing of the Treaty, the Irish Free State came into existence. From February 1922, the Provisional Government took responsibility for education affairs. At an early stage, the Free State indicated its general support for continuing with a denominational system of education. For example, teachers were to be trained at denominational training colleges. In 1924, the Department of Education was established. The Free State continued to demonstrate that 'the principles of education in the historic practice of the Catholic church were the trusted guidelines for an Irish education policy.'[1] The Free State did, however, introduce education legislation. The School Attendance Act 1926 made attendance at school compulsory for children aged between six and fourteen years. (The upper limit was raised to fifteen years in 1972 and to sixteen years with effect from 2004.)

The primary education sector developed with primary schools (state-aided, though owned by the churches) and state schools (including special schools which provide for children with special educational needs and *gaelscoileanna* vested in the Minister for Education and Science).

The impetus for the development of **special schools** came from a landmark Report of the Commission of Inquiry on Mental Handicap 1965, which provided a framework for subsequent developments in special education. At the end of 1967 there were already in operation sixty-two special national schools catering for five main categories of children and they described these categories as: blind and partially sighted; deaf and severely hard-of-hearing; mentally handicapped; physically handicapped; emotionally disturbed.[2] Current government policy is that a child with special educational needs is to be educated in an inclusive setting, unless this is not in the child's interests or there are very good reasons why it is not practical (Education for Persons with Special Educational Needs Act 2004).

The 1970s saw the question of multi-denominational education receiving attention. Parents who were interested in this issue came together and in 1978 the first **multi-denominational** primary school was founded in Dalkey, County Dublin (the Dalkey School Project). It was state-funded and independent of church control and was managed by a limited company without share capital. It led to the establishment of a body called Educate Together. As additional multi-denominational schools were founded, they became members of Educate Together, which reserved a veto over policy decisions to each member school.[3] Because the multi-denominational schools cater for children with no faith and those with many different faiths, they are likely to grow in number in what has been identified as an increasingly multi-cultural Ireland.

The 1970s also saw a group of parents gather together to support primary teaching through the medium of the Irish language and they established a co-ordinating body called **Gaelscoileanna**. Its objectives were to help parents to set up *gaelscoileanna* and to safe-guard the Irish medium schools in existence. The Department of Education and Science buys the site and builds the new schools and the schools may opt for either diocesan patronage or the patronage of a nationwide body called An Foras Patrúnachta na Scoileanna Lán-Ghaeilge (which is a limited company). Like the multi-denominational schools, the *gaelscoileanna* are increasing in popularity and are likely to continue to grow in number. (Second-level schools that offer tuition through the medium of Irish are identified in Appendix B).

Developments in the twentieth century: second-level education

There are currently four types of second-level school: secondary schools; vocational schools (sometimes called community colleges); community schools; and comprehensive schools (see fig 1.1. overleaf). This section will trace the development of these types of school.

Secondary Schools

Secondary schools (or voluntary secondary schools as they are properly called) remained the main provider of second-level education from 1922–1960.[4] They tended to be 'academic' in ethos and they prepared pupils for the Intermediate (now Junior) Certificate and Leaving Certificate Examinations. In most of these schools, pupils paid fees (though payment was at the school's discretion). The Intermediate Education (Amendment) Act 1924 introduced the payment of capitation grants to schools for each recognised pupil and, with this first step towards involvement in second-level education, the State claimed a small measure of control. This control increased with the introduction of State capital grants in 1964 and what became known as 'the free education scheme' in 1967.[5] Most secondary schools joined the scheme, while some remain outside it to this day. (Appendix B indicates whether schools are fee-paying or not).

Secondary schools constitute the largest school type. Nationally, over half the post-primary schools are secondary schools and they educate

Fig. 1.1
Overview of provision of second-level schooling in Ireland

TYPE OF SCHOOL	MANAGEMENT	FUNDED BY
SECONDARY SCHOOLS	• Privately owned/ managed • Majority conducted by religious communities • Some conducted by Boards of Governors or by individuals	• State pays over 95% of teachers' salaries • Secondary schools in the free education scheme also get allowances & capitation grants
VOCATIONAL SCHOOLS & COMMUNITY COLLEGES	• Administered by vocational education committees • Vocational education committees are statutory bodies	• State pays up to 93% of total cost of provision • Balance is provided by receipts generated by the vocational education committees
COMPREHENSIVE SCHOOLS	• Board of Management which represents the following: the VEC of the area, the Minister for Education and Science and the diocesan religious authority	• Fully financed by the Department of Education and Science
COMMUNITY SCHOOLS	• Board of Management which represents local interests	• Fully financed by the Department of Education and Science

PARTICIPATION & PROGRAMMES TAUGHT	FEES
• Approx. 55% of all second-level pupils attend secondary schools • Academic subjects (tradition of academic education) • Technical and practical subjects now offered in many secondary schools	• No tuition fees in approx. 91% of all secondary schools as they are in the free education scheme. • Tuition fees charged at remaining 9% of secondary schools; fees vary from school to school; the fees at boarding schools may be significantly higher than those charged at day schools (see Appendix B)
• Approx. 30% of all second-level pupils attend vocational schools • Academic subjects: wide range of academic subjects available • Technical & practical subjects offered in all VEC schools (tradition of teaching manual subjects and of preparation for trades)	• No fees
• Academic subjects: wide range of subjects available • Technical & practical subjects: wide range offered	• No fees
• Academic subjects: wide range of subjects available • Technical & practical subjects: wide range offered	• No fees

more than half of the second-level students. Almost all secondary schools were denominational from their foundation: most of them were founded by religious communities serving a predominantly Catholic population, with the remainder founded by lay people serving Protestant and minority religions and by individuals. In the past the principals and, in most cases, the teachers in Catholic schools were members of their founding religious orders. Similarly, in Protestant schools and schools run by other denominations, the principals and staff were usually members of those churches. Due to the decline in the numbers of religious brothers, sisters and priests, this has changed and today management and staff are predominantly lay people in all Catholic schools. The management of secondary schools is provided by Boards of Management or Boards of Governors. The schools remain in private ownership and reflect the ethos of their foundation. Over 95 per cent of the cost of teachers' salaries is met by the State, with the balance met by the individual school that employs them (see Fig.1.1). In addition, in schools where no tuition fees are charged (i.e. 91 per cent of secondary schools), the State pays allowances and capitation grants (for every pupil enrolled in the school).

Traditionally, secondary schools provided an academic type of education but in recent years they have tended towards the provision also of technical and practical subjects. Most of the Catholic schools were single-sex schools at the time of their foundation, but a number have become coeducational in recent years, either through amalgamations or to meet the needs of the area in which they are located. Many more secondary schools offered boarding facilities in the past than do so now. The social and economic factors contributing to the decline in boarding schools are beyond the scope of this short background history, but they include the increase in the number of second-level schools throughout the country, the improvement in transport, including that provided directly by the Department of Education and the decline in the number of religious sisters, priests and brothers to staff the Catholic boarding schools. Because the Protestant population is in the minority and more geographically dispersed, members of those churches, who wish their children to be educated in Protestant schools, are more likely to have to send them a distance from home and, consequently, the option of boarding is sometimes favoured.

Vocational Schools

As mentioned earlier, a framework for technical instruction emerged after the legislation of the late nineteenth century. This was further developed after the Vocational Education Act 1930 with the formation of vocational schools. The state owns these non-denominational schools and provides the cost of the school site, buildings and all renovations. At the time of their introduction, the original intention was that these schools would concentrate on the development of skills in areas such as woodwork, metalwork and practical subjects, as well as literacy and numeracy. Pupils were prepared for the Group Certificate examination. At that time, they would have left school when they reached the minimum school-leaving age and progressed to apprenticeships in the trades, or to work in local industry and agriculture.

After 1963, post-primary education included a common Intermediate Certificate for pupils at both secondary and vocational schools. Vocational schools now offer the full post-primary programme of courses to Leaving Certificate.

The passing of the Vocational Education (Amendment) Act 1970 facilitated the development of community colleges. These are either newly-established, or restructured from existing vocational schools. They are similar to community schools, but with a different management structure and are operated under the care of the vocational education committee of the local authority.

Vocational schools and community colleges comprise the second largest school type. They constitute approximately one-third of all second-level schools and educate almost 30 per cent of all pupils. The state provides 93 per cent of their total cost, with the balance coming from the vocational education committees themselves. No fees are paid by parents. They provide the full range of second-level courses and prepare their students for the same public examinations at Junior Certificate and Leaving Certificate levels. Vocational schools educate boys and girls together. They have a particular commitment to lifelong learning and provide evening and daytime courses for adults in the community they serve. Many of them also offer post-Leaving Certificate courses (PLCs).

Comprehensive and Community Schools

So, from the 1930s until the 1960s the second-level system was divided into two distinct school types: secondary schools which offered an academic education on the one hand and vocational schools, emphasising technical and practical subjects, on the other. The 1960s in Ireland was a decade of major educational change, brought about by a shift in government policy away from what was increasingly being seen as a divisive or selective system towards a unified or integrated one. Comprehensive education was perceived as a way of achieving that unity and integration. The Minister for Education of the day commented: 'I do not anticipate that the number of public comprehensive schools will be very great. My aim is that secondary and vocational schools, by the exchange of facilities and by other forms of collaboration, should make available the basis of a comprehensive system in each locality'.[6] The first state-run, comprehensive schools in Ireland opened in 1966. Meanwhile, the Department of Education continued to work towards a new model of second-level school – to be called a Community School.

In October 1970, the Department of Education issued a document entitled 'Community School'. It was so revolutionary that the Minister had to clarify, in reply to Dáil questions, that it 'was in the nature of a working document, not a circular. It brought together, in a form suitable for discussion, my ideas as to how what I had in mind could be achieved by the establishment of community schools.'[7] He also had to clarify that these schools would be established 'in areas where under existing arrangements educationally viable post-primary schools could not be established.'[8] The intention was to reassure the secondary school providers and, indeed, the vocational school sector, that the new schools would not be set up in competition with them. This development in government policy was a logical step from the provision of free post-primary education in 1967. Its stated aim was 'to provide reasonable equality of educational opportunity for all our children irrespective of the area of the country in which they reside or the means of their parents.'[9] These schools were formed through amalgamations of existing secondary and vocational schools thus providing a better use of personnel and facilities. Also, in some cities and suburbs, new community schools were built, with their management board reflecting educational and community interests.

Special education

There are no second-level special schools; all special schools are under the Department of Education and Science Primary Branch. In practice this means that some pupils aged twelve years and over remain in or transfer to special (primary level) schools. Current government policy is to include pupils with special needs in mainstream schools, as far as possible. Its stated aim is to educate those with special needs:

> ... in an inclusive environment with those who do not have such needs, to provide that people with special needs shall have the same right to avail of and benefit from, appropriate education as do their peers who do not have such needs, to assist children with special educational needs to leave school with the skills necessary to participate, to the level of their capacity, in an inclusive way in the social and economic activities of society and to live independent and fulfilled lives.

> *Education for Persons with Special Educational Needs Act, 2004*

School size

Over half of the second-level schools are secondary schools; one third are vocational schools and community colleges; the rest are community and comprehensive schools. The largest schools are in the community and comprehensive sector, with an average enrolment of 580; the smallest are the vocational schools with an average of 400 per school; in between, the average enrolment for a secondary school is 470 (see Table 1.1). As with all averages, these figures mask internal differences: there are very small and very large secondary schools and vocational schools. However, there are no very small community and comprehensive schools.

Table 1.1
No. of full-time students in post-primary schools aided by the Department of Education and Science (2004–2005)

School Type	Number of Schools	Number of Students
Secondary	403	184,526
Vocational	247	98,641
Community & Comprehensive	92	52,443
Total	**742**	**335,610**

Data source: www.education.ie

The emerging trend in Irish education is for schools to become larger. In some cases this is due to the amalgamation of smaller schools to create a school with over 500 pupils enrolled. Almost 300 schools have an enrolment of over 500 pupils, while less than 100 schools have an enrolment of under 200 pupils (see Table 1.2).

Table 1.2
Post-primary school size in 2003–2004

Less than 50 pupils	9 schools
50 – 99 pupils	21 schools
100 – 199 pupils	65 schools
200 – 299 pupils	118 schools
300 – 499 pupils	239 schools
More than 500 pupils	291 schools
Total	**743 schools**

Data source : www.education.ie

What is the structure of second-level education?

The programmes on offer and the public examinations for which second-level students are prepared, are given in more detail in Appendix A. The structure can be summarised as follows (see Fig.1.2): a three-year **Junior Cycle**, followed by a two or three year **Senior Cycle**, depending on whether the optional **Transition Year** is taken.

Fig.1.2
Structure of second-level education

Programme	Junior Cycle	Senior Cycle
Duration	1st Year 2nd Year 3rd Year	Transition (4th) Year (optional) 5th Year 6th Year
Courses	Junior Certificate Junior Certificate School Programme (JCSP)	Leaving Certificate (established) Leaving Certificate Vocational Programme (LCVP) Leaving Certificate Applied (LCA)

The **Junior Cycle** reflects the view that students should be exposed to a wide range of educational experience at this stage of their development. The programme is delivered over three years and pupils are assessed either by the Junior Certificate or the Junior Certificate School Programme (see Appendix A). It is hoped that, when they have completed it, they will be able to proceed to senior cycle with confidence or, as is the case for a minority of Irish students, leave school at the minimum school-leaving age with the requisite skills and knowledge for adult life.

Transition Year follows the Junior Cycle. It is widely regarded, by both parents and schools, as one of the more enlightened developments in Irish second-level education. It comes immediately after students have sat their Junior Certificate examination and provides them with an opportunity to experience education for its own sake. There is no public examination at the end of Transition Year. Instead, students are awarded certificates by their school for different areas of achievement. They are also awarded a Department of Education and Science certificate. They build up a portfolio throughout the year and, as they accumulate learning experiences, they record their achievement in their portfolio.

The portfolio may also contain certificates awarded by external bodies such as professional institutes. Transition Year students frequently develop a mini-company during this year and also get involved in projects which raise their social awareness, either within their local community or for developing countries. Their portfolio will reflect the diversity of their activity throughout the year.

During the final two years of their schooling **(Senior Cycle)** students take one of three Leaving Certificate programmes.

All post-primary school types provide programmes or courses which are prescribed by the Department of Education and Science and they all prepare pupils for the public, externally marked, examinations. However, not all schools deliver the full range of certificate programmes. When you read about the range of programmes and examinations in Appendix A, you may be able to form some idea of the programmes which might best suit your child.

For example, if you feel your child will need the full six years in second-level education, in order to reach a level of maturity which will allow her to function well in third level and the world of work, then you will be looking out for schools which offer **Transition Year** at least as an option. Or you might look for the **Leaving Certificate Vocational Programme (LCVP)** as this offers the possibility of pursuing Leaving Certificate examination subjects combined with work experience and other vocational features of Transition Year. Either the LCVP or the **established Leaving Certificate** is necessary for entry to third level; the **Leaving Certificate Applied** prepares candidates for direct entry to the world of work.

For details on post-primary programmes and examinations, turn to Appendix A.

Enrolment

So, having looked at the schools in your area, how do you go about enrolling your child in the school of your choice?

There is no central enrolment system, so you should approach the school directly to enrol your child. As schools may not have a place for every applicant, they may use a selection process. The Education (Welfare) Act, 2000, 19 (1) states:

> The board of management of a recognised school shall not refuse to admit as a student in such school a child, in respect of whom an application to be so admitted has been made, except where such refusal is in accordance with the policy of the recognised school concerned published under section 15(2)(b) of the Act of 1998.

That reference is to The Education Act, 1998, section 15 (2)(b) of which requires the Board of Management of a school to:

> ... uphold ... the characteristic spirit of the school as determined by the cultural, educational, moral, religious, social, linguistic and spiritual values and traditions which inform and are characteristic of the objectives and conduct of the school.

Section 15 (2)(d) of the Act requires the Board of Management to publish:

> ... the policy of the school concerning admission to and participation in the school, including the policy of the school relating to the expulsion and suspension of students and admission to and participation by students with disabilities or who have other special educational needs and ensure that as regards that policy principles of equality and the right of parents to send their children to a school of the parents' choice are respected and such directions as may be made from time to time by the Minister, having regard to the characteristic spirit of the school and the constitutional rights of all persons concerned, are complied with.

Because of the statutory obligation outlined above, the admissions policy is to be found in all school literature and/or on the school website.

In practice, this means that the first criterion for enrolment is that the applicant lives in the school catchment area (see Appendix B). Where the number of applicants exceeds the number of places available, other criteria may be introduced. Typically, these would be 'sibling already in the school' or 'attends the junior feeder school'. Under the Act, schools are entitled to apply these criteria so long as they are published and available to applicant parents.

School fees

As indicated in Fig.1.1, all community, comprehensive and vocational schools are free of tuition fees. Of the secondary schools, 91 per cent are free. This means that the number of schools charging fees is very small. (For every school in Appendix B we have indicated whether it is free or fee-paying). Even among boarding schools, some fall within the free scheme, so they charge fees to cover the cost of accommodation only, but no tuition fees.

Whether a school is free or fee-paying, parents have to face costs. These may include school books and stationery; school uniform; sports equipment; and fees for public examinations. There may be additional expenses such as music lessons, sports training, school meals, educational outings and school trips (abroad or within the country). In some schools parents organise a book exchange system and a second-hand uniform sale. In designated schools, the Department of Education and Science supports a book scheme and a food scheme.

In order to supplement the funding received from the Department of Education and Science, it is common practice among schools to ask parents for a 'voluntary contribution'. However, schools may not insist on payment and, in practice, compliance with this request for payment varies from 40 per cent to 80 or 90 per cent. Schools may also look for a deposit in order to secure a place. This is intended to discourage parents from 'multi-booking'. When parents book their child into several schools, it makes it extremely difficult for schools to plan, as they do not know until the school opens in September whether the child is coming to their school or not. To overcome this difficulty all the schools in an area sometimes hold their enrolment sessions on the same day.

Progression to third-level education, training and work

The Central Applications Office (CAO) is an agency that is independent of the school system, the universities and the institutes of technology. It is designed to give school leavers the best possible chance to achieve entry to the **higher education** course of their choice on the basis of their performance in the Leaving Certificate examination. Six Leaving Certificate subjects are taken into account for this purpose: 100 points are awarded for an A1 in a subject, so 600 points represent maximum points. In January each year, the Sixth Year students complete a form for the Central Applications Office, indicating the courses they would like to take in order of preference.

When the Leaving Certificate results come out in mid-August, the CAO informs the candidates which courses are available to them. This is referred to as the 'offer' and the candidate has to respond, accepting, in order to ensure a place on the designated course. It follows that the more demand there is for a course, the higher the level of points required to achieve entry to it. Students have an idea from the previous year(s) what the points level for the course of their choice is likely to be and consequently whether it is realistic to apply for it. It makes sense, of course, for candidates to aim a little higher than their past level of success. Indeed, a burning desire to gain entry to a particular course can have the effect of raising a candidate's results right across the board.

In addition to higher education (provided by the universities and institutes of technology), there is also **further education** including many post-Leaving Certificate (PLC) courses. Application is made directly to the colleges of further education. These courses lead to awards from the Further Education and Training Awards Council (FETAC). They are of value in themselves and also because they can be used as 'rungs' in the 'ladder' system which governs educational progression all the way from the Junior Certificate to postgraduate awards. Many of these colleges also offer programmes leading to awards from various professional bodies.

Some schools develop close links with local industry, for example through work experience programmes as part of Transition Year and the Leaving Certificate Vocational Programme and these may result in companies taking past pupils as soon as they have finished in second level. Also, various combinations of work experience and training are available to school leavers particularly in the service, hospitality and retail sectors, through FÁS and Fáilte Ireland among others.

Guidance and Counselling

The education system may seem complex and even daunting. However, there is help available. A very important resource in Irish schools is the guidance and counselling service. It starts before the child leaves primary school and continues throughout her second-level education, with advice and support appropriate to the stage she is at. As Brian Mooney, President of the Institute of Guidance Counsellors, has noted, the service will help children to:

> Develop and accept a whole picture of their talents and abilities; to grow in independence and develop their ability to take responsibility for themselves; to make well-informed choices about their lives and to assist them to follow through on those choices.[10]

Summary

The educational system can be traced back to some key developments that took place in the nineteenth century. The Catholic religious orders and the Protestant voluntary societies continued to play a pivotal role in its development throughout the first half of the twentieth century by founding and running secondary schools. Vocational schools were introduced in the 1930s. The 1960s was a decade of great educational change, that resulted in free second-level education being introduced as well as the first comprehensive and community schools. Today, second-level schools offer a three-year junior cycle leading to the Junior Certificate examination and a two or three-year senior cycle leading to the Leaving Certificate examination. A wide range of subjects is available. Application is made directly to the school. Some parents apply to several schools as demand may exceed the number of places available in any one school. Fees are payable in a small number of schools. Every school is required to 'use its available resources … to ensure that students have access to appropriate guidance to assist them in their educational and career choices.' (Education Act, 1998, 9.d). The service is delivered through professionally trained guidance counsellors who also deal with the problems that adolescents may experience in their personal and social lives.

2 Choosing a school
What research tells us

In this chapter we will identify some issues that are important to parents who are choosing a school. These include: matching the child to the school and using networks and the grapevine to gather information. The chapter draws on interesting information from the UK and the USA.

What is important to parents?

There has been little published research on parental choice and schooling in Ireland. However, the subject has been examined extensively in the UK. While this book is a guide for parents in Ireland and not a sociological study, a broad outline of UK research can alert us to issues that emerged as particularly important for parents.[11] For example, parents in the UK indicated that they used 'the grapevine' to help them select schools.[12] In this book, Irish parents are also seen to rely on 'the grapevine' so it is necessary to examine its use. Secondly, in the UK research we found areas that were sufficiently common to the Irish situation that they helped to define the limits of our research.

Matching your child to a school

Studies have shown that some parents, by virtue of their own experiences, are more likely to 'imagine' a particular future for their child and even to have a goal in mind such as a specific profession. They engage in 'matching' their child to the school that they see as being able to provide the education to achieve this goal. Parents who engage in 'child-matching' are likely to choose a school that suits 'the particular proclivities, interests, aspirations and/or personality of their child.'[13] The needs and talents of the child are of great interest to parents who believe the 'best' school is the right school. For such parents, gaining insider knowledge of the school system and researching schools, is of great importance.

For other parents, matching is 'more generalized ... [and] related to ... the child's happiness or ability to cope or flourish at school and to more general future possibilities.'[14] These parents are interested in everything from school size, subjects offered and uniform, to school reputation.[15] However, while some families expressed great concern that their children should get a 'good education', due to the competing pressures of work and family life, they tended to opt for the seemingly 'obvious and appropriate' school.[16] The local area was of importance to these families: mothers could meet their daily responsibilities within a support network that included their neighbours. Sending a child out of the local area to school would have involved dealing with transport and re-organising family routines and childcare.

At the same time, other parents thought that sending a child to the nearest local school was almost like making 'no choice' at all and making 'no choice' seemed irresponsible. They believed that trying their best to match their child to a particular school was part of their duty as parents. Some parents are prepared to go to great lengths in order to achieve this kind of matching. If they are 'confident about their children's ability to manage travel' then they will not be put off by the fact that the school is outside their locality and they will make safe travel plans for their children.[17] Other parents, who were unwilling to engage with the 'unfamiliar', favoured schools close to home.[18]

So, what are the important factors for parents who do engage in trying to match their child to the 'right' school? Again, looking at existing research before we consider the Irish context, there are useful studies that point out what parents value in schools. Research indicates that factors 'such as safety of the school, standards of discipline and opportunities for sports and extracurricular offerings affect parents' choices.'[19] Reputation and image emerge as being of importance to parents. Image could be linked to the wearing of a uniform and the conduct of pupils in public places. Reputation could be linked to something specific: the school had a 'reputation' for sport, or art, or good examination results. However, studies show that parents are concerned with more than facilities and examination performance tables. They are concerned with the behaviour and activities in the school and with the conduct, character and manner of its students.[20] In both the UK and the USA, research has shown that academic achievement is of less importance to parents than school ethos and climate.[21] In many instances, it is most important that the child should 'want to go' to the school chosen by the parent, while some parents prioritised 'good discipline' and other parents had 'a fundamental commitment to the private sector.'[22]

Hearing about schools on 'the grapevine'

There are many different reasons for making a choice of one school over another where choice exists. Research done in the UK in the 1990s includes an examination of how parents use 'the grapevine' to get knowledge about schools in order to make an informed choice. Grapevine knowledge is passed via social networks, local groups and informal gatherings where parents exchange information, rumour and gossip. Almost every one of the 172 parents who were interviewed made some reference to having drawn on the 'impressions and experiences of friends, neighbours and relatives in their choice-making.'[23] This kind of networking is very much a part of the complex way that people relate to each other. But grapevine knowledge is not always based on accurate information and it often results in making parents feel uncertain about their decisions. This is particularly so because school reputations are vulnerable to change over time and so-called 'knowledge' that is passed on the grapevine can become dated and unreliable. Parents are using knowledge that is passed as rumour and rumours tend to be used to fill in missing information or to explain the seemingly inexplicable. Despite the fact that information passed in this way is unreliable, parents seek it out and sometimes view it as more useful than 'official' information, especially information provided by the schools themselves.

Families who participated in the research for this book had a strong awareness of the grapevine and the pervasiveness of rumour, indicating that some parents in Ireland use networking and social contacts to gather information about schools. Parents often favour personal recommendations of schools, given by other parents in close contact with the schools. They see this as being more trustworthy than information that has been constructed to guide parents, such as school prospectuses, lists of school activities and information on examination results. The tendency to favour rumours, recommendations and grapevine knowledge is no doubt linked to parents' desire to penetrate the 'official' front of schools and somehow really see inside them in order to make an informed choice. In a sense, parents are viewing each other as valuable sources of information and their shared position as parents inclines them towards mutual trust. The grapevine is therefore a 'powerful way in which parents can circumvent professional control over information and the resulting selective public presentation.'[24] When analysing grapevine knowledge, research indicates that it is not evenly distributed across parents and access to such knowledge is determined by 'where you live, who you know and what community is open to you.'[25] However, grapevine knowledge can suffer the fate of the 'information' passed in a game of Chinese whispers. The more often it is passed on, the less accurate it can become.

Exchanging information about schools

Getting information from other parents is time-consuming and requires access to the relevant network of parents. Research shows that men have less access to the grapevine than women and that information mainly passes between women. Often information is exchanged around primary schools and neighbourhoods and mothers – whether or not they are in paid employment – tend to engage more frequently in this kind of social gathering. Mothers who have lived for some in the area surrounding the school often know other mothers (of older children) who have already made decisions about second-level schools. In one UK survey, a mother articulated very clearly how she believed parents could use their primary school 'network'. She emphasised that 'if you're fairly active within a school, you [will] know parents ... you have got to be the one that keeps the finger on the pulse ... and one very good way of doing that is if you're on the PTA [Parent Teacher Association].'[26] By and large, research shows that 'in most families of whatever form or structure, the mother has, or shares, the main responsibility' for choosing schools for the children.[27]

Indeed, 'ensuring children's educational success becomes the personal responsibility of the mother. And ... mothers rather than fathers [assume] this responsibility on a day-to-day basis.'[28]

In our research for this book, we asked parents – mothers and fathers – if they were involved in their primary school PTA and, if so, why they had become involved. As we shall see in chapter five, they were aware of the PTA as a useful network and a way of getting closer to the whole 'inside' culture of the school. We also questioned school principals on how they viewed Parent Associations and parental involvement and examined second-level school prospectuses to see how parental involvement continues into second-level education. While some parents view literature such as the school prospectus or handbook as containing 'cold' knowledge and the information passed on the grapevine as 'hot' knowledge, it is important to use official school literature to gain an understanding of school characteristics such as ethos and values.[29]

Perhaps the most significant point to emerge from studies of 'grapevine knowledge' about schools is that parents were often swayed by what they heard. To some degree, they wanted the confirmation of other people's approval because they were uncertain about their own judgement. The danger is that in doubting your own judgement, you begin to privilege the judgement of another parent and, therefore, support someone else's choice. But information passed along the grapevine is not always based on direct knowledge – rather, it is 'pseudo information.'[30] In chapter five, we will examine how Irish parents used informal 'grapevine knowledge' and how they sourced information directly from the schools they were considering for their child. We shall see that the 'right' school for your child may not be the one you heard favourably talked about in the locality and that your needs may differ significantly from those of the other parents in your neighbourhood.

Summary

While there is little information on school selection and school choice in Ireland, these topics have been researched in depth elsewhere. Research has identified common concerns for parents who are choosing a second-level school for their child. Firstly, these studies have shown that not all parents really think about choosing a school. For reasons including cost, travel and family priorities, many parents send their children to the nearest school and do not consider other options. Even where there are no difficulties with cost/travel, many parents favour the local second-level school anyway. This can be because it has a 'good' reputation, and/or because it is a popular choice for families whose children have already attended primary school together.

Secondly, where parents engaged deeply in making a 'choice' of second-level school, they had confidence in their own abilities to find enough information in order to make a reasoned and informed choice. Parents used both official sources of information (prospectus; website; school open day). They also sourced information from people with 'inside' knowledge when possible and they used local networks and the grapevine to gather information.

3 What makes a good school good?

School choice is an under-researched topic in Ireland, but there is a considerable amount of Irish research in the areas of academic outcomes (results), subject choice, school environment, streaming/ banding and school size. In this chapter we look at these areas and also comment on discipline, teacher expectation and school management

Results and league tables

The notion underlying 'league tables' is that the school with the best results in public examinations is the best school. According to this method of ranking schools, the best results are the highest results in terms of points for entry to third-level education. But as a way of measuring the effectiveness of schools and comparing them with each other in order to select the best school for your child, this is fundamentally flawed. First of all, it ignores the pupil intake.

For instance, in a league table, the 'top' school may be a relatively small one, which cannot take all applicants. Or, the 'top' school may be a very large school, which does take all applicants and which has six class groups in its final year. Here, the Sixth Year will be more or less representative of the population and the very high results will occur in about one-sixth of the cohort. Even in terms of crude examination results, then, the more interesting question to ask is not, which school got the highest results? The pertinent question is, how much did the school contribute to the results? In short, league tables will tell you less about the school than you actually need to know in order to make an informed choice. You may wish to consider issues that have been found to have a direct impact on children's experience of school. These issues include school type, school environment, subject availability and choice, streaming and banding, discipline and teacher expectations.

School type

Research indicates that many factors are involved in the 'delivery' of good examination results, but that school type is not one of them. It is unlikely that a parent, in a particular geographical location, will be presented with a choice between all school types: secondary, vocational and community or comprehensive. However, the programmes and examinations offered in second-level schools are broadly similar across all school types. Nevertheless, our research revealed a perception among parents that one school type might be in a position to 'deliver' better examination results than another and they were keen to choose the school which would give their children the best chance of achieving their full potential. However, from her analysis of Junior Certificate results, Emer Smyth could conclude that 'school type ... tells us little about differences between schools in average examination results.'[31] Instead, a number of schooling factors influence the outcomes and these factors are examined below.

School environment

A school is an extremely complex organisation. In Chapter Six we will refer to the values and ethos statements, found in school literature, which indicate how the schools will play a role in the lives of their pupils. The sheer range of goals expressed there is an indication of the scale of the task which schools have set themselves in order to provide the best possible learning environment for their pupils. Factors identified in international research as influencing pupil outcomes include: social context; school management and staffing; school organisation and class allocation; school climate; teacher effectiveness. Emer Smyth's study takes this multidimensional view of school effectiveness and tests it in the Irish context. Her study focuses 'not only on academic outcomes but also on absenteeism and drop-out [rates] and on aspects of personal/social development among pupils.'[32]

For the purposes of this book and its aim to help you choose a school which will be the best school for your child, Smyth's research is useful in that it shows the influence of schooling factors on outcomes – social, developmental and academic – for the pupils. The second part of her research, involving a case study of six schools: two 'academically more effective'; two 'academically less effective' and two 'average' schools, gives a more detailed report of these, including interviews with principals, vice-principals and staff. It is interesting to note that 'Improved academic and non-academic outcomes are closely associated with certain aspects of school practice.'[33] We shall look at some of those aspects of school practice now.

Subject choice and class allocation

One of the aspects of second-level schooling, which can confuse parents, is the bewildering array of subjects on offer and the near impossibility of making a selection if the child has no prior knowledge of the subject, particularly if it is not possible for the child to first experience the subject in question. The second related issue is how pupils are grouped in classes (class allocation). Even if all the schools being considered make broadly comparable curricular provision, schools may vary significantly in the way in which subjects and subject levels are made available to pupils. It has been found that more academically effective schools 'tend to be more flexible in relation to choice of subjects and subject levels, delaying a final decision in order to maximise the number of pupils taking higher level subjects.'[34]

In these academically effective schools, first year might offer a 'sampling' system whereby pupils have an opportunity to try out a wide range of subjects for periods of time ranging from two weeks to two months. After sampling a range of subjects, pupils select the ones they are going to take for their Junior Certificate. The decision about which pupils will take the higher paper and which pupils will take the ordinary level paper can be left as late as Easter of third year in these schools.

The size of the school has a direct impact on those decisions. Table 1.2 in Chapter One shows that, for the school year 2003/2004, there were thirty schools with an enrolment of less than one hundred pupils. In other words, there was just one class of less than twenty in each year of a five-year cycle. Furthermore, there was a total of ninety-five schools with an enrolment of less than two hundred which, with a six-year cycle, would indicate the possibility of one class certainly in some of the years. In some of these schools, the practice is to teach pupils of all levels together (mixed-ability teaching) until the point where additional tuition needs to be given to the weaker pupils in preparation for the state examinations at foundation or ordinary level and additional material needs to be covered with those taking higher level examinations.

Such mixed ability teaching becomes increasingly more difficult as the range of ability widens. In a large school, the range of academic ability is more or less reflective of the population and school management has to take serious decisions as to how best to deal with this range of academic ability, in order to get the best out of each individual and allow them all to achieve their full potential.

There are four grouping options open to schools:

- streaming
- mixed ability
- banding
- setting.

Streaming is the grouping of pupils by academic ability. They are assessed, either before or just after their arrival in the school and their performance in that assessment test decides the class they will be in. However, most schools do not stream that rigidly in first year and many postpone any such decision until the following year. **Mixed ability** teaching is often used in first year with incoming pupils being assigned to a class randomly, in alphabetical order of surnames for instance. Many schools use the assessment test results, not to segregate pupils into different levels of academic ability, but in order to ensure an appropriate mix in every class group. **Banding** is the system most used in the larger schools. This system is essentially a mix of the previous two, without being as extreme as either. It uses test results to divide pupils into broad ability bands. So, in a typical year group of one hundred and fifty pupils, there would be three bands divided on the basis of academic ability.

Then, within those bands, pupils would be subdivided into class groups on the basis of mixed ability. **Setting** means grouping pupils by ability in certain subjects. Most usually the 'set' subjects in schools are mathematics, English and Irish. The pupils are then in mixed ability groupings for their other subjects.

Most schools use a mixture of these systems. Mixed-ability grouping is the most popular practice at school entry, even where streaming or banding is introduced in preparation for the Junior Certificate examination.[35] As Drudy and Lynch have noted, 'It is usually asserted that schools stream because they believe strongly that it is in the interests of the students to do so.'[36] For example, those who support the use of streaming tend to argue that it leads to better outcomes for most pupils.[37] They believe that, in a mixed-ability class, highly able pupils may be 'held back by being grouped with slow learners' while less able pupils may suffer because of 'constant comparisons with higher-performing pupils'.[38] Schools make parents aware of their class allocation system and their reasons for adopting that system.

Discipline

The Board of Management is required to prepare a code of behaviour specifying

- the standards of behaviour that shall be observed by each student attending the school;
- the measures that may be taken when a student fails or refuses to observe those standards;
- the procedures to be followed before a student may be suspended or expelled from the school concerned;
- the grounds for removing a suspension imposed in relation to a student; and
- the procedures to be followed relating to notification of a child's absence from school.

Education (Welfare) Act 2000 Section 23

The principal is required to issue that code to parents before registering their child as a student. Schools usually publish their code of conduct in their prospectus and/or in other school literature such as the homework journal. It sets the tone for student behaviour and, by requiring parents to sign it, the school effectively includes the parents in the issue of what is expected of their child in terms of discipline. One principal we interviewed stressed the importance of the family sharing the school's regard for appropriate behaviour: 'If it's not regarded as important at home, we are wasting our time trying to enforce it here.' The stated value, common to many of the school discipline codes which we reviewed, is respect. Pupils are expected to show respect for the property of others, including school property; for the views of others, including those of different cultures and belief systems; for the personal integrity of others; and respect for themselves, highlighting the need to have an environment in which students can learn without interference. This disciplinary climate requires quite detailed systems, which are drawn up by the principal in consultation with staff, parents and, in some cases, pupils. They include monitoring pupils' punctuality and homework, as well as their behaviour involving staff and other pupils. The success of these systems will depend, not so much on their design and publication, but on their implementation in a clear, consistent and fair manner. Unsurprisingly, research indicates that the more academically effective schools are characterised by 'a consistent application of school rules and procedures along with relatively early involvement of parents in disciplinary procedures.'[39]

Teacher expectation

Our research for this book indicated that parents did not put 'good teachers' very high on their list of priorities when choosing a school. This might seem surprising, given the pivotal role of the teacher in the level of interest a child is likely to take in a subject. However, in our interviews with parents, a more nuanced response to that question became apparent. First of all, it is clear that we have in this country a very well-qualified teaching profession. In that sense, parents simply took for granted that the teaching staff would be good. They felt that there is, broadly, no inherent difference between teachers in the different schools they were considering for their children. In addition, their common sense told them that there is a variety of teaching styles and that pupils respond differently to different teachers. What they were hoping for, however, was that their child would be encouraged, given positive feedback, given a sense of achievement and self-worth. The research would suggest that they are on the right track here. Pupils who feel that their teacher expects them to do well, generally do well: 'The level of teacher expectations within a school (as perceived by pupils) has a positive and significant impact on pupil performance.'[40]

In our interviews with them, teachers expressed their belief that the brighter pupils will do well in any school. They saw their role as being far more important for their less academic pupils, to encourage them and build their self-confidence in order to ensure that they did as well as they possibly could in the examinations which would have such an impact on their choices in the future. What is important is that the potential of the child is fulfilled. In this regard, it is interesting to note that, according to Emer Smyth's research, schools vary more in the academic performance of lower ability pupils; in other words, schools make more of a difference for this group.

We indicated at the start of this section that 'success', in terms of the 'best' school, is based on a number of different factors and so, a school where this high level of teacher expectation exists will 'also tend to be characterised by a more flexible approach to subject choice, a stricter disciplinary code and more positive interaction between teachers and pupils.'[41]

Management

There is quite wide variation between schools in the way in which they are managed. Theoretically, the management structure is the same in all schools: all have a principal, one or more deputy principals and additional members of staff in posts of responsibility. And yet, how they interact, the frequency of formal meetings, the quality of informal contact, the style of communication of decisions to staff and students, the extent to which they form a real management 'team' and perform the management role, is far from uniform across schools:

> Less academically effective schools appear to be characterised by less staff involvement in decision-making in the school, less emphasis on formal staff meetings, less positive relations between management and staff and less supportive relations among colleagues.[42]

There are certain statutory obligations that apply to all principals. However, the way in which the principal works with the management team, the teachers, the parents, the students and the ancillary staff, differs between schools. An important factor here is school size. The principal in a school of a few hundred pupils and twenty to thirty staff will clearly have a different daily experience of the management role from a principal in a school of over a thousand pupils and seventy to eighty staff.

School size

In our research, we asked principals whether they felt there was an optimum school size. One indicated that once the systems were in place the school either worked or it did not and this was not related to its size. On the other hand, several principals suggested that the optimum size was around six hundred pupils. The reason for this response is related to resource allocation by the Department of Education and Science. They reckoned that, with six hundred pupils, a school can make good curricular provision, have sufficient teachers eligible for management roles and still be sufficiently small that the school community is experienced as a cohesive one by all those involved and that there is a feeling among its members that they know one another. It might be of interest to parents to know that, in terms of pupil performance in the Junior Certificate Examination, school size was found to have no significant impact.[43] However, in terms of their child's happiness and sense of self, school size could be important. There is no doubt that certain personality types, who might feel stifled in the small school atmosphere, would thrive in the less intimate but perhaps more varied surroundings of a large school. Other children might feel lost or even alienated in a large school and these might be happier in a smaller school.

Summary

The lesson to be learned here is that examination results cannot be taken in isolation. Even if academic achievement is your number one requirement of the school, you should look for a school with the characteristics that are most likely to provide the best environment for the development of your child. If the school can provide an ordered, safe environment, where your child is encouraged and supported, where his talents are nurtured and his achievement is praised, then the examination results issue will take care of itself. You need to be aware of the commitment of the school to the various aspects of your child's education.

Schools vary in the way in which subjects and subject levels are made available to pupils and research has indicated that academically effective schools tend to be flexible in relation to choice. Aside from the issue of subject choice, parents may want to become familiar with how pupils are grouped in classes (class allocation). Parents should also become familiar with what is expected of their child in terms of behaviour so that they can support the disciplinary environment of the school. Good disciplinary procedures are linked to effective schooling, as is teacher expectation. But it is important to note that:

> Schools are rarely exceptionally 'effective' or 'ineffective' across the whole range of pupil outcomes, a pattern that makes the identification of broadly effective schools more difficult. In addition, the imprecision involved in ranking schools even in relation to one particular outcome, such as academic performance, means that a 'league table' approach is inappropriate.[44]

4 Single-sex or mixed?

Parents are sometimes confused by what they hear about the relative merits of single-sex schools and mixed schools. In this chapter we will look at what some studies have found. The chapter will give information on issues such as examination results for boys/girls and Leaving Certificate performance in single-sex and mixed schools. Finally, the chapter will comment on co-education and personal/social development.

What are the main differences?

The development of community and comprehensive schools and community colleges has increased the provision of co-education and in addition many secondary schools have moved from being single-sex to being co-educational. The result is that the traditional choice offered to parents in the past, between 'the nuns, the brothers and the tech', is changing.

It is important to point out that, contrary to widely held beliefs, there are no significant differences discernible in Leaving Certificate examination results which can be ascribed specifically to co-ed or single-sex schooling.

Parents we spoke to explained to us how they chose schools for their sons and daughters. A belief that was articulated by a number of parents is that 'girls do better in single-sex schools' (see Chapter Five). In further teasing out this point, it became clear that these parents were referring to outcomes in terms of Leaving Certificate results. Their view was that examination results for girls are better in single-sex schools than they are in mixed schools. Let us look at the two realities of the Irish education system: the breakdown of schools by gender mix and the examination results of boys/girls. This may help you to come to an informed decision about why you would prefer a single-sex or a mixed school for your child.

Single-sex schools and mixed schools: how many are there?

We addressed the historical evolution of the education system in chapter one and saw that the Catholic Church provided for the education of the majority of the population in secondary schools, with priests and brothers educating boys and religious sisters educating girls. The remaining secondary schools are run by Boards of Governors on behalf of the Church of Ireland and other minority religions. A number of these were coeducational from their foundation, but others have always been single-sex schools.

This meant that single-sex schools remained the almost exclusive form of education on offer until the Vocational Education Act in 1930.

After the Second Vatican Council in the 1960s, religious orders changed the way in which they looked at their role in society. This resulted in some religious sisters, brothers and priests moving out of education and into other social work. In addition, some of the areas where secondary schools were established have undergone demographic change, with the result that enrolments declined. In order to ensure that these schools would not close down completely, boys' and girls' schools were amalgamated.

So, in a secondary sector that was almost exclusively single sex, the balance between single sex and co-educational is changing significantly and quite quickly. In the Department of Education and Science listing for 2004–2005, out of a total of 403 schools in the secondary sector, 148 are co-educational. Of the single-sex schools, 111 are boys' schools and 144 are girls' schools (see Table 4.1).

Table 4.1
Secondary Schools by Gender

	Number of schools	Percentage of total
Single Sex boys	111	27%
Single Sex girls	144	36%
Co-educational	148	37%
Total	**403**	**100%**

Data source: www.education.ie

Fee-paying schools and free education

Another related way in which Irish second-level education differs from most of its international counterparts is the cost to parents. Traditionally, secondary education in Ireland was fee-paying and continued to be so until 1967. After that date, some secondary schools opted to continue to remain outside the 'free scheme' and they are fee-paying to this day. So, when comparisons are made between single-sex and mixed, it is important to be aware of the other differences which exist between school types.

Vocational schools provided free education from their foundation in 1930. They were mixed schools although, in the early years, boys and girls were often taught separately because of their subject choice: boys took technical subjects and girls took domestic and clerical subjects. Vocational schools were founded to address a different educational need and did not, for instance, offer the Intermediate Certificate (now Junior Certificate) and Leaving Certificate examinations for their first thirty years. Partly arising from the emphasis on technical subjects, although they were mixed schools, more boys than girls attended them. In 1981–82, for instance 73 per cent of girls in post-primary education were in secondary schools and only 18 per cent were in vocational schools, whereas the comparable figure for boys was 60 per cent in secondary schools and 30 per cent in vocational schools.[45]

Comprehensive schools, which were introduced in the 1960s and Community schools in the 1970s, are largely co-educational and are also free. Although some of these were new schools, many of them were formed through an amalgamation and expansion of existing secondary schools. There are 88 mixed schools in the community and comprehensive sector and 4 single-sex schools (see Table 4.2).

Table 4.2
No. of Community/Comprehensive and Vocational Schools by gender

2004–2005	C & C	Vocational
Single Sex boys	2	1
Single Sex girls	2	3
Co-educational	88	243
Total	**92**	**247**

Data source: www.education.ie

So, overall, across all school types, almost 65 per cent of schools are now coeducational with just 35 per cent single sex. In the past, most Irish people were educated in single-sex schools and you may have benefited from what single-sex schooling had to offer. However, the reality now is that more schools are mixed, so as a parent you probably have a wider choice for your child than your parents had for you.

Examination performance

The important point for you as a parent is that in this country we have moved from a position where the majority of schools were single-sex to one where the majority of schools are mixed. The speed of this change makes it very difficult for the parent to come to any meaningful conclusions about single-sex versus mixed schooling. However, parents commonly perceive that there is a connection between single-sex education and good examination performance and they have the impression that research bears this out. The fact is that, even twenty years ago, Irish research was not making this connection. In 1986, an analysis was done of the Leaving Certificate results of girls and boys in Irish, English and mathematics in co-educational and single-sex secondary schools.[46] Brennan found that in all three subjects the performance of girls in co-educational secondary schools was higher than that of girls in single-sex secondary schools. The differences were greatest in Irish and mathematics. Brennan's conclusions are as follows:

> When social class is controlled for, as it is to a certain extent in comparing secondary schools only, we find co-education to have no adverse effects on girls' performance within this sector. Indeed, the opposite seems to be the case. Girls in co-educational secondary schools do better than girls in all other school types in Irish, English and mathematics.[47]

On the other hand, contrary to the beliefs expressed by parents, Brennan found that boys in single-sex secondary schools performed better than boys in co-educational schools. However, Drudy and Lynch have noted that 'this is not surprising in view of the fact ... that boys' secondary schools were more socially selective and more academically oriented in pupil culture than other secondary schools.'[48]

Table 4.3
Pupils taking Leaving Certificate in 2004

	LC including LCVP	LC Applied
Boys	26,311	1,748
Girls	28,911	1,772
Total	**55,222**	**3,520**

Data source: State Examinations Commission

Table 4.3 shows the number of girls and boys that took the Leaving Certificate (including LCVP) and the Leaving Certificate Applied in 2004, while Table 4.4 gives the Leaving Certificate results for the year 2004, indicating the achievement of girls and boys. It can be seen clearly that a higher number of girls than boys sit the examination; a higher number of girls achieve the minimum five passes (D3) and a higher number of girls achieve at every level above that. Table 4.4 does not differentiate between those attending single-sex and those attending coeducational schools. It simply demonstrates the superior performance of girls in the Leaving Certificate examination nationally. Every year when the examination results are published, this phenomenon attracts media attention. Ireland is not alone in this. Similar concern about the low achievement of boys is expressed in the UK, the USA, Australia and, increasingly, other countries across Europe.

Table 4.4
Gender Differences in Aggregate Leaving Certificate Results 2004

Achieving	Girls	Boys	Girls %*	Boys %*
TOTAL	28,911	26,311		
Minimum 5 D3s any level	26,215	23,752	91	89
Minimum 6 D3s any level, of which minimum 2 C3s or higher on higher papers	17,451	14,310	60	54
Minimum 6 D3s any level, of which minimum 4 C3s or higher on higher papers	12,286	8,675	42	33
Minimum 6 C3s or higher on higher papers	6,615	4,015	23	15
Minimum 6 C3s or higher on higher papers of which minimum 3 B3s or higher	5,915	3,557	20	14
Minimum 6 C3s or higher on higher papers of which minimum 3 A2s or higher	1,927	1,188	7	5

Data source: as published in the State Examinations Commission annual report 2004

* rounded up for easier reading

The underlying reality about the different examination performances of boys and girls is more complex than at first appears. In order to examine the issue in more depth, the National Council for Curriculum and Assessment commissioned research into gender and achievement in the Junior and Leaving Certificate Examinations.[49] The report confirms many of the points we have reported from other research in chapter three, namely, that multiple factors contribute to differences in examination performance such as 'teaching and learning in classrooms, school organisation and culture, teacher expectations and perceptions of students learning.'[50]

Coeducation and Leaving Certificate performance

So, having looked at the examination results for girls and seen that they are higher than for boys, can we say whether 'girls do better' because they are in single-sex schools?

The historical development of the different school types in the Irish system continues to have an impact on the type of pupil who enrols. Traditionally, secondary schools were single sex, fee-paying and perceived as 'academic'; vocational schools were co-educational, free and perceived as 'technical'. The development of community and comprehensive schools and community colleges, has increased the provision of coeducation and, as indicated earlier, secondary schools themselves have been moving from being single sex to being coeducational. Research undertaken in the 1990s concluded that attending a mixed school had no direct bearing on Leaving Certificate results.[51] Equally there is 'no clear evidence to suggest that merely organising boys and girls into pre-defined sex groups is going to help their school performance.'[52]

What about co-curricular activities?

Other differences exist between single-sex and coeducational schools, which have an impact on the pupils both in terms of outcomes at the end of their schooling and in terms of their happiness during their school years. The parents we interviewed were very keen that their chosen school would not be one-dimensional focusing exclusively on examinations, but that their children would experience a range of co-curricular activities. Many schools now have long-established traditions in different areas of activity. Frequently, these are associated with the founding religious order, or even with a particular teacher. Evidence of participation and success in different areas of endeavour will be clear to a parent reading the prospectus and visiting the school. Some schools have as a requirement that every child belongs to at least one team, society or other co-curricular activity to complement their academic study.

There are differences even within the secondary school single-sex sector between boys' and girls' schools in this regard. In a study of the 'ethos' of girls' schools, Kathleen Lynch made important observations on some of the differences between girls' and boys' schools. For example, she found that in girls' schools a commitment to academic achievement was evident through the frequency and compulsoriness of assessments and, the 'achievement ethos was frequently stronger than in boys' schools.'[53] While girls' schools placed greater emphasis on personal development and self-discipline, boys' schools placed a high priority on sporting achievements.

Coeducation and personal/social development

Some of the parents we interviewed were educated in single-sex schools. They suggested that some of their social and personal shortcomings, particularly with regard to relationships with the opposite sex, were a result of their single-sex education. This made them wonder whether their children would benefit both socially and personally from the more 'natural' co-ed environment. They were committed to raising their sons and daughters in a spirit of gender equality. They hoped that their children's schooling would support them in this commitment. They selected a co-ed school because they believed that a mixed education would help their children to adapt to the changing roles of men and women within the family unit and that they would have less 'traditional' views of men's and women's work. It has to be remembered that while schools are committed to the holistic development of their pupils, 'personal / social development among pupils is likely to be subject to a very broad range of influences, including family circumstances, neighbourhood effects, peer groups (outside school) and so on.'[54]

Summary

In Ireland there was a long tradition of single-sex education which was related to the involvement of Catholic religious orders in schooling. Although there are still single-sex schools, 65 per cent of second-level schools are now mixed and there is provision for coeducation across all school types: secondary, vocational, community and comprehensive. This means that parents have more choice, but they can become confused when they hear conflicting comments on the relative merits of single-sex and mixed education. For example, an issue of interest to parents in our study was whether or not girls 'do better' in single-sex schools. Contrary to widely held beliefs, there are no significant differences discernible in Leaving Certificate examination results which can be ascribed specifically to attendance at co-ed or single-sex schools.

5 Making a choice
Parents' voices

In this chapter, we give you the views of parents on a range of issues that were important to them when choosing a school. These issues include: school reputation and environment; the advantages of boarding school; and choosing different schools for siblings. Parents also comment on the importance of using your instinct when trying to select the right school and becoming involved in the school that your child eventually attends.

Which school is right? Using your instinct

Having information about schools greatly helps parents to make an informed choice about the best one for their child. In our research, we found that both educators and parents shared the view that the best school for a particular child is the one that facilitates that child's social and academic development, in an environment that is safe and nurturing. If you are trying to create a good match between your child and a school, then you need to think as much about your child as about the contents of the school prospectus, or the anecdotes about the school that you have heard. Most schools are very accommodating about providing information – indeed sometimes parents can find it impossible to make a choice between several schools which appear, from their literature, to be fairly similar. Typically, schools send out a prospectus; they invite parents to an Open Day, at which they may involve some older pupils to answer questions. Many schools also encourage prospective parents to visit the premises and take a tour of the classrooms. These are all opportunities for parents to allow themselves to consider their 'instinctive' response to the schools.

However, many parents find it difficult to trust their instincts as to whether or not a seemingly 'good' school will suit their child. In one UK study of school choice, Catherine Itzin argues strongly that parents should visit any school to which they are considering making an application and they should trust their first impressions as well as assessing the information provided by the school.[55] By way of experiment, she visited thirty-eight second level schools before making any applications for her son who was in primary school. She graded the schools on a scale of 1 to 10, based on her impressions of the overall atmosphere and how she felt about the way each school dealt with key issues (such as discipline, equal opportunities, subject choice, academic standards and parental involvement). Undertaking this kind of exercise requires that you place more trust in your own instincts and impressions than in hearsay, publicity and crude measurements of 'success' such as league tables. You will have to try to see the school as your child will see it and imagine whether or not your child will thrive in that school's environment. Allowing how you 'feel' to influence your decision is courageous.

Some parents interviewed for this book indicated that they had a 'gut feeling' about certain schools, where they knew their children would not fit in. In some cases, parents indicated that they wanted a school 'with a good academic reputation'. However, they trusted their instincts: they knew what their children were really like and the kind of environment that would suit them best and in some cases the 'right' schools were not particularly academic. For example, Parent D said that the key concern for himself and his wife was to select a school that would make their children 'happy'. Happiness was mentioned by most of the parents in this study, but they had different ideas about what would bring their children happiness. For Parent D the most important thing was that his three children would 'integrate' well when they went into second-level schooling. He chose the same community school for his two sons and daughter and, as it happened, they were all happy there. Their expressions of 'happiness' were different though: his daughter simply 'felt the place was made for her' and settled totally; his sons were very happy in certain classes and were generally content at school.

Parent F's instinct about the right school for her children was based on her awareness of the particular strengths and vulnerabilities of each child. She pointed out that she had chosen a school with a strong emphasis on academic work for her older son, because 'he's quite bright and he really thrives with a bit of encouragement and a bit of a challenge'. On the other hand, she thought it was unlikely that this school would suit her younger son, who was not particularly academic and was less out-going. Having done some research into a smaller school in the area, she concluded that it might suit her second son. Her judgement was based not only on her formal enquiries, but also on her instinct about her children. It was influenced by vague feelings, likes and dislikes, all of which are part of the instinctive response: '[This school is] much smaller ... you know the teachers can see who [the kids] are ... and I suppose I like small schools as well, because I know all the kids as well and I can sort of – well, I think I know more about what's going on.'

Happiness was the guiding principle for Parent J, who said that 'the Leaving Certificate results of a school and their academic achievements wouldn't be as important to me as the child's welfare and well-being. I'd rather have a happy child'. Her four children had different interests, abilities and strengths, yet she selected the same all-Irish secondary school for all four. She did so because her instinct told her that the school had the atmosphere and characteristics that would allow them to develop to the best of their ability. While her third child was less academic than his older brothers, she believed that the small size of the school – and having his siblings at school with him – would outweigh any disadvantages associated with being at a school with a strong academic reputation. Her instinct informed her view that 'he could get lost in a big city secondary school. If he's going to struggle, he might be better struggling in a small secondary school, surrounded by people he would know and a language that he would be very familiar with'.

Happiness was also identified as crucial by Parent N, who believed that, once she found a school with the right 'environment' and 'community spirit', then everything else would fall into place for her son. Her instinctive response was crucial to her decision-making process: 'I felt that if my child is happy in the [school] community then all other features of school life would follow easily for him: his academic development, his social development, all of that'. Like the other parents above, Parent N kept the particular needs of her child clearly in view. The idea of community spirit and a 'caring' environment were important to her for reasons which she outlined: 'My son is an only child and I felt it was even more important ... that he would be looked after and cared for ... Education is about more than results and academic achievement, so I chose a school for him to help him to grow and develop.'

While parents often allow their instinct to tell them which school is best for their child, it is important to remember that children change considerably during their teenage years. The school selected for a twelve-year-old, may not suit the child as he grows into adolescence. His interests and strengths may become much more obvious later and parents may even consider moving the child to another school if it is a better 'match' for the child. Some of the parents in this study were pragmatic about this possibility. Parents K said that in choosing a school for their two daughters (currently in primary school), they read up on five Dublin schools. They then settled on two that were close to home and filled out application forms for these schools. Their research led them to conclude that one of these schools has 'a strong academic record', but this was not the most important factor for the parents: 'We looked for a school that might match and rise to meet the girls' academic ability. And if we feel that is not going to be the most important thing for the children, if their strengths turn out to lie elsewhere, we might not use [the academic record of the school] as our number one criterion.'

For some parents, the availability of support within the school for the special educational needs of their children was crucial in the decision-making stage. Parents X sent their three daughters to a single-sex secondary school. Their decision about a school for their son changed when they found that the school of their 'choice' could not facilitate his special needs. They were keen that he should attend a mainstream school and commented: 'We were involved in a Parents for Integration scheme, where children with special needs would go to a mainstream school ... we set about going to try the different community colleges and one [community college principal] said he'd give it a go.' Their son thrived in the school and the parents were particularly happy with the atmosphere of caring in the school. Indeed, second only to the 'happiness of the child', the 'caring' atmosphere of the school is of particular importance to parents.

A caring environment

Without doubt the teachers and principal are central to the development of a caring environment. This is evident to parents. Parent C stated: 'Caring stems from the Principal'. But, she noted, teachers can also show a willingness to help pupils who are troubled. She selected different schools for her children, but placed a priority on finding schools that signal to the pupils that 'if you need to talk, someone will be there. If you have a problem, there will be someone. The size should have no impact on this – it's there or it isn't.'

Parent C felt strongly that parents need to know that they have picked a school where they 'know that their children are going to be monitored' – a school that 'cares if someone's going astray and parents will be notified'. But she argued that the spirit of caring must spread among the pupils themselves. 'The pupils must know that [the school] is a safe place – that each pupil has a responsibility to care'. Other parents defined aspects of the caring culture of schools as being present in different forms.

Parent F chose different second-level schools for her two boys. Her younger son was quiet and not athletic. For Parent F, the right kind of 'caring' was manifest in a school that had 'a slightly gentle approach [to academic work]'. The school was small (<400 boys) and she believed that her younger son would have got lost in the busyness of the large school (>900 boys) that she had chosen for her older son. She believed that a school, small or large, could show that it is 'caring' by acknowledging different skills in pupils.

> 'Most important is that they encourage them in all directions … if one child is good at art, encourage that direction, if another is good at maths but bad at something else … [a caring] school should recognize it … Like, a lot of kids go to school and they're great at story writing … but they think they're bad at maths and science … but if they were encouraged to think they weren't bad, then in many instances they'd overcome those problems.'

Parent F made her choice of a small school for her younger son on the basis that it might be more caring. Parent F shares a widely held view that it is impossible for very large schools to provide a culture of care. Parent K said that she had attended a small school (<400 girls) and commented that 'a lot of what I want for them is what I had and they probably won't get, which is, a very caring and human environment.' While she wants her daughters to attend a school 'where there's a caring attitude and approach', she observed that the second-level schools in her area are large (>800 pupils) and concluded that 'maybe the size of school will rule that out.'

Some parents identified very specific forms of 'caring' evident in the schools they had chosen for their children. Parent J had recently separated from her husband and their children were adjusting to new living arrangements while still going to school every day. Parent J found the school very supportive. As she noted, there are children of either separated or single parents in every class in the school and it is not a 'big deal' in a general sense. She believed that her children experienced a high level of care during a difficult time and that the teachers were 'aware' yet not intrusive. Equally important to Parent J was the fact that the school principal listened very carefully to the details of the separation and the new domestic arrangements and was supportive of Parent J over a long period of time.

Parent N needed a different kind of 'caring environment' for her son. The family lived in an isolated area of rural Dublin. Because her son had no siblings, she wanted a school where he would be embraced into a lively and stimulating environment. She chose a school in the centre of Dublin on the basis of its stated ethos of caring. A short time after her son started at the school, her family circumstances changed: 'My husband died when my son was twelve years old and the school, I have to say, took over a whole role at that time ... it became a very important home to him.' She felt very strongly that her initial choice had been vindicated.

So, what can you do to determine whether or not a school has a 'caring' environment? A small school has the attraction that the pupils and parents will all 'know' each other. However, it is important to note that school size is not a predictor of a good school atmosphere and small schools are not necessarily 'better' education environments. Small schools (< 400 pupils) do not necessarily have small class sizes or a lower pupil-teacher ratio. In a large school, with a big staff, it may be possible for the Principal to manage resources in such a way that the class sizes are not large. It is also likely that a large school (> 800 pupils) will have sufficient staff to offer a wider subject choice than may be possible at a small school.

In addition, resources such as computer and science facilities, engineering and technology rooms, gymnasium, playing fields and a wide range of co-curricular activities are more likely to be available at larger schools. It is important to ask about class size, subject range and facilities, when enquiring about a school as these will all contribute to the overall atmosphere. Whether their school was small or large, the over-riding concern of the principals we interviewed was to provide a safe and caring environment for their pupils.

The reputation of the school

Parents also emphasised the importance of the 'reputation' of the school. They are often influenced by the views of neighbours and friends and seek out whatever kind of 'local knowledge' of a school is available. As noted in chapter two, researchers in the UK have referred to this as 'grapevine knowledge'. It is often passed between mothers who know each other through neighbourhood networks, or who meet around the primary schools. Mothers who already have older children attending second-level schools are sometimes viewed as reliable sources of grapevine knowledge.

When speaking with families in Ireland, we found that there was a strong awareness of grapevine knowledge, but some parents expressed caution about relying on it. Parent F was very aware of local knowledge about the schools to which she had made applications for her two sons: 'certainly on the boys' side I've heard good things about [the two schools] definitely. Being a small school. Like, teachers do excellent work with the kids – very much an environment of helping them to do well, to do better.'

This kind of grapevine knowledge was particularly important for parents who indicated a preference for schools with an academic emphasis and parents who had long-term plans for their children that included university education. Parents Y work within the education profession and said that this made a difference to them, as they had easy access to 'insider' and local knowledge and they were able to discriminate between useful and irrelevant information. Parent Y said: 'I would know the schools and the reputation of the schools and I would know that [the ones I have applied to] have a very high rate of transfer to university which would be a key issue for me'.

For Parent F, academic reputation was also very important and she be-lieved that around her area in Dublin some schools had developed academic reputations that made them highly desirable. She commented frankly: 'This whole secondary school thing is a cat fight. Everybody's trying to get into the same schools. At the end of the day, there probably are enough places for all the kids, over all the schools. But everybody seems to be chasing the same ones … it creates a highly competitive situation.'

Other Dublin parents expressed similar views. Parent Z linked the reputation of schools directly to a 'high level of transfer to university' and said that while this 'shouldn't probably be the most important thing, it is for me'. Nonetheless, she also expressed a degree of cynicism about grapevine knowledge:

'Well, you don't know anything about a school, do you, so it's all hearsay. Short of sitting in a lesson, you haven't the foggiest idea. We put [our eldest] down for [a private school]. For all I know, it could be absolutely hopeless. But from what I hear, it seems to be a fairly OK school.'

She concluded with a view shared by many parents who have to make a choice:

'I'd like to spend a day in a school to see what it's really like. I mean, you hear awful stories about a school, then you hear the opposite. It's a shot in the dark. You're taking a big chance.'

Her view that choosing a school is 'a shot in the dark' was shared by Parent K, who said she had 'relied heavily' on the views of other mothers she knew through the primary school network and eventually placed her daughters' names on the waiting lists of two schools in her area. Despite having listened to the opinions of others, she observed:

'What you perceive to be the right school before they start school can only be known [about] in retrospect. Anecdotal evidence of the school or perhaps family and friends' experience of that school, is never going to be the same as your own experience.'

When considering schools, it has to be remembered that a 'reputation' is not fixed: reputations change. A change of school principal sometimes precipitates a change in reputation. A school can enjoy a period of growth and development. A school can be situated in an area of population decline and its 'reputation' may simply be a consequence of demographic change.

It is also important to weigh up the actual value to your child of a school's reputation: if your child has ability in mathematics and sciences and indicates a clear interest in scientific study, then it is important to ascertain whether or not the school you are considering can offer a range of science subjects through to Leaving Certificate level.

The school may have a 'reputation' for being small and friendly, or for being very progressive and unusual. If these are characteristics that appeal to you, then you may have to forget the image of a school that you favour and select one that meets your child's interests. Similarly, if a child is simply not interested in the traditionally academic subjects, then you should consider schools which offer alternative programmes (see Appendix A) and ignore hearsay about academic schools being the 'best' schools. It is simply not the case that a high rate of transfer to university implies that a school is intrinsically 'good'. As Parent K said, a school is only good if 'it serves your children well and they do well in it and develop and flourish'. The common-sense approach of Parent K is shared by many parents, teachers and school principals:

'Go with your instinct. Try to find somewhere that suits your child. It is a huge decision to make on the basis of hearsay.'

Single-sex or mixed?

As noted earlier, much research – internationally and in Ireland – has been done on pupils' experiences and performance in single-sex and mixed school environments. You may find that reading the overview of such research in chapter four helps to unravel some of the confusions about the debate over the relative merits of single-sex and mixed school-ing. In Ireland, despite the changes outlined in chapter four, we still have a significant number of single-sex schools. In Western Europe, co-education expanded from the 1950s and was generally perceived to be a more 'natural' environment for pupils as it reflected the mixing of the sexes that is part of both home and social life. However, some parents have held on to the view that single-sex education is better and, in particular, they seem to believe that it is better for girls.

In our study, several parents had a strong impression that girls 'do better' in single-sex schools. Parent K said that she would consider only single-sex schools for her daughters and had no interest in examining any mixed schools:

> 'I've no hesitation in saying I would like them to go to single-sex [schools] for secondary school ... I think it's fairly understood and established that girls just don't perform to their best in mixed [schools].'

She associated single-sex schooling with higher academic achievement than mixed schools. However, she conceded that 'if it turned out that the child wasn't doing particularly well [academically] ... it may be that the mixed school might have other things to offer, which might be good for the child's development.' In Ireland, the 'other things' that a mixed school (such as a community college or community school) might have to offer could include subjects not usually offered to girls in single-sex schools, such as engineering and technical subjects.

The school climate was a factor for parent J, when she chose a mixed school for her sons. However, she was still vaguely aware of common perceptions about the disadvantages that mixed schools might have for girls:

> 'People say girls don't do as well in a mixed school as boys do.' She attributed this to the distractions that a mixed environment includes and thought that boys did not succumb to distraction as easily as girls: ' ... as teenage [girls], once you fell in love you didn't think of anything else except the person you're in love with. Whereas boys are different, more removed, so they can cope.'

For Parent J, part of the attraction of a mixed school for her sons was that it made them relaxed and open about issues such as relationships and sexuality: 'It does make them very open, they're very open about a lot of things,' she concluded. However, for Parent Z, the presence of girls in the class presented the possibility of 'distraction' and she chose to send her sons to a boys' school. Much as Parent J had thought that girls 'fell in love' and couldn't concentrate in mixed schools, Parent Z figured that boys did too and therefore didn't apply to a nearby community school. She commented: 'I wouldn't want him to be distracted by girls and I know that happens to a lot of kids. There's a lot of lovey-dovey and fancying goes on at [the local co-ed school].'

The possible distractions of a mixed environment were also noted by Parent F who had ruled out the school nearest her home on the grounds that she wanted single-sex schools for her sons and daughters. She had an idea that research supported her position:

' ... some of the research I've heard about, certainly from the States, they always talk about [in the] single-sex schools the kids do better ... Socialising can happen, you know, outside of school and later on.' She favoured single-sex schooling as the optimum environment for academic development and wanted to be able to monitor their involvement in mixed-sex social activities: 'We do youth clubs and, kind of, football clubs and tennis clubs and all that sort of thing, so we'd be putting them into more supervised mixed environments.'

Parents' concern about their adolescent children being distracted by romantic relationships is not unreasonable. In part, parental concern may reflect the fact that many Irish parents over 40 years of age were educated in single-sex secondary schools (see chapter one) and they may have transferred fears and concerns onto their children out of their own ignorance of the mixed educational environment. Such fears are not always groundless and sometimes adolescents do find it hard to concentrate on schooling when also dealing with emotional involvements with class-mates. Adolescents can experience intense emotions but may be ill-equipped, through sheer lack of maturity, to deal with them. Indeed, sometimes it is not so much the relationship itself, as the difficulty of coping when the relationship ends. The young people still have to see each other in school every day and this can prove very difficult if one of them is feeling rejected.

Teenagers are not immune to adolescent crushes and to falling in love, while attending single-sex schools and educating girls and boys in separate schools is not going to remove the possibility that relationships will develop during adolescence.

Many parents consider that a mixed school is the more 'natural' environment, as it mimics real life. Others opt for the nearest school and if it happens to be a mixed school – so be it. Parent D never gave a thought to the fact that his two sons and daughter were going to be in a 'mixed' school when he sent them to the local community school. He opted for the 'same choice for all' and it 'didn't even occur' to him to separate the children and send them to single-sex schools. However, he always kept a close eye on how happy his children were and how involved they were in school activities.

It seems perfectly reasonable to assume that children will do very well in mixed schools as long as they settle and are not inhibited by, or distracted by, the opposite sex. By keeping an eye on your children as they settle into second-level school and by encouraging them to bring new friends home regularly, you are more likely to be aware of any problems or tensions as they arise. By reading some of the research on the debate about mixed and single-sex education, you may come to see that the 'differences' are not so significant that they should cause concern to most families (see Chapter Four).

Parental involvement in the school

In Chapter Two, we looked at research which has indicated that parents use 'the grapevine' as a source of local and sometimes 'inside' information about schools. Some parents believe that becoming involved in their children's schools – both primary and secondary – can give them a kind of 'insider' knowledge. An involvement in a primary school Parent Teacher Association (PTA) may provide contact with parents who already have older children attending second-level schools and they may have opinions and advice worth considering. Involvement in the Parents' Association of the second-level school that you choose may help you to get close to school issues and give you a platform to express ideas and opinions.

The Parents' Association is often a fund-raising body, but fund-raising is rarely its only function. Most Parents' Associations are concerned with supporting the delivery of the curriculum and creating a communication route between teachers and parents. Sometimes they organise parenting programmes and talks for parents on relevant home/school issues. They are also a good social outlet and a great way to meet other parents. The Education Act includes among the functions of a parents' association to '(a) advise the Principal or the board on any matter relating to the school ... and to (b) adopt a programme of activities which will promote the involvement of parents, in consultation with the Principal, in the operation of the school.' (Education Act, 1998, subsection 26). So, their brief is quite wide; they have real advisory as well as consultative powers and provide a very useful vehicle for parent involvement.

Families who co-operated with this research had different views on the importance of the Parents' Association to them, though all indicated that they were generally supportive of the schools attended by their children. A few parents were supportive in a more formal way, either by membership of the Parents' Association, or by being elected to the school Board of Management. They had different reasons for becoming involved in a structured way. In some cases the involvement was 'strategic'. For example, one family had returned from living in the USA for three years and their four children were re-entering the Irish education system.

Parent F considered that it would be important to 'get involved in the school and find out what was going on'. Her reasons reflected her desire to develop good 'insider' knowledge of the system and to increase her ability to manage and monitor her children's schooling. She commented: 'I wanted to be involved in how the school worked. And I wanted to know about the decisions being taken, to know why things were happening. Decisions being made by the teacher body. And knowing the teachers involved.' While her involvement with the PTA included co-ordinating some social events, fundraising and providing direct support to co-curricular activities, she was also privy to the kind of knowledge that 'impressed' her children: 'I used to get a lot of kudos from my kids, because I could say I know all these things about school. They thought I was up there with the principal. We would know Board of Management decisions, slightly ahead of the main body of parents. We would be – consulted is too strong a word because we wouldn't alter the decisions – but we would be informed about the decisions that the Board of Management had taken.'

For Parent J, joining the PTA of her children's primary school and eventually the Board of Management, was both a chance to get to know the school and a new social network. Her involvement began with the primary school that her sons attended and she valued the views and opinions of other parents that she met through the school. Her experience with school committees gave her huge insight into the education system and directly influenced her choice of second-level school for the children. Parent J served on the PTA for ten years and the Board of Management for six years. These are long periods of service, but she explained that 'the school was small and they didn't have an awful lot of parents going forward'. In addition, once she was elected parents' representative on the Board of Management (for two terms) she automatically had to stay on the PTA. She was happy to devote a lot of energy to the school committees, but initially felt disappointed that so few parents were similarly committed: 'Other parents are happy to drop them at the school gate, would be my opinion. From experience, when there's an AGM, there'd be twenty parents at it and there could be over a hundred families in the school.' Parent J accepted that some parents couldn't volunteer much time, adding: 'As a mother who stays at home, it was nice to have that way of getting out and meeting people. Other people who'd be out at work all day wouldn't thank you to have to get up and go out again to a parents' meeting. That's totally understandable.' In addition to the social element, Parent J joined the committees in order to 'get a good insight into the school and see what's going on and what will be going on. It was one of the best ways of doing that really, to get involved, to get to know teachers and the principal.'

Getting involved in school committees sometimes means having to seek out information and put oneself forward for election. In a large school, new parents often feel that it would seem 'pushy' to want to join the Parents' Association and they prefer to hold back for a year or two. It is worth considering the benefit to you and your child that could be gained from early involvement in school committees or in voluntary support work. It will help you to understand the school organisation and culture better and may confirm that you have made the right choice for your child. In addition, it will help you to choose confidently for another child. It will also give you a chance to 'give something back' to the school – a point made by several parents. Parent N did not join any committee attached to her son's second level school, but she did a lot of voluntary work for the different charities with which the school and the pupils were involved. She opted to 'make this contribution through the school ... to show my son that it was important to me and that it wasn't just something that I expected him to do but that I too was involved. And the school just plain needed help at the time. They had various projects and work to be done and I had some time.'

On the whole, parents seem to benefit from the additional contact with schools that is afforded by committees such as the Parents' Association and Board of Management. There are different ways of becoming involved in committee work and different election systems in schools, so it is worth asking about this. Pupils sometimes bring home information about an AGM on a flyer or newsletter that never leaves the schoolbag. You may need to remind your child to give you messages and notes, read the bulletin board in the school and ask other parents if they have heard of any meetings coming up. Your level of involvement could develop into an important interest – indeed this is often how parents first hear of the National Parents Council (Primary and Secondary) and about professional organisations that may be of help to the child. For specific details about your school, you should contact your Parents' Association or the parents' representative to the Board of Management.

Should the school be near home?

For some families, travelling a distance to and from school every day is simply not possible. There may be cost implications involved in such travel and where children are travelling alone each day there may be concerns about safety. For many families there are logistical issues involved in getting children to their schools, particularly if parents work outside the home and have to commute. An added difficulty is co-ordinating school travel where more than one school is involved. For example, one child may have moved to second-level education while another is still going to a national school.

It is worth thinking about second-level schooling as early as when you are deciding on a primary school. The fact that national schools are not 'feeder' schools with links to specific second-level schools may make them less attractive to parents who want to send their children to the same school from Junior Infants through to Sixth Year. This kind of school, which will probably be single-sex, may suit parents who want to drop their children off in the morning and know that they are within the same school grounds all day.

Some of these schools have after-school clubs for the junior classes so that they can stay on the school campus until early evening and be collected with older siblings. Many of them have after-school activities or homework clubs for the older pupils also. A school with these facilities may be particularly attractive to working parents, who want to feel assured that their children are in a safe, supervised environment all day. However, primary schools outside the national system are fee-paying and they usually 'feed' to their own fee-paying second-level school. They are also very few in number. Parents need to consider how affordable such schooling is and then weigh it against factors such as the cost of travel to a free school and the cost of other types of after-school child-care.

For many parents, the attraction of a community school or community college may be that it is right in the centre of their locality and children can walk to and from school with their friends. Such schools also usually have after-school activities such as sports. The availability of supervised homework clubs and the cost of such clubs, varies from school to school. Parents cannot assume that all schools in Ireland stay open after school hours, or that they offer supervised care after school hours.

If after-school care is the deciding factor for you, make sure that you have discussed provision with the school. This is a service that is often initiated and, indeed, sometimes provided by the Parents' Association. It is unlikely that such a service will be offered during mid-term breaks and official holidays. Parents who work outside the home usually plan additional child-care for school holidays and for older children it has become very popular to go to summer camp (residential or non-residential), to Irish college or, indeed, to language schools or family homes in Europe.

The advantages of sending your child to a school near home include short travel (therefore less tired at the end of the day) and school friends are likely to be neighbours. The kind of 'surveillance' that parents like to do with teenagers is easily accomplished if their children socialise with others from the neighbourhood and travel short distances to school and social activities. Families who spoke with us had different opinions on the value of a school that is 'near to home'. Parent C stated simply that she 'didn't believe in travelling distances' to get to school. With five children, it would have been a logistical nightmare to have co-ordinated different travel times and routines. Parent C also had strong views on the importance of a 'local' school: 'Once homework is done, there should be time for other things. If they are travelling distances from school, other things can't be done. You must belong to your locality, be part of the local community. If all the kids are being bussed in and out [to school], the neighbourhood becomes a very isolated little place. There'd have to be something majorly wrong with the local school to travel a distance.'

Parents G sent their children to schools within walking distance of home. When three of the older children were teenagers, they went to a boarding school. The younger ones always walked to school. It was a practical decision:

'Because we had such a large family, it was important that the school should be near home. I knew people who were spending their days driving children to and from school and we wanted to avoid that. In the event, it also meant that their friends lived nearby.'

Other families with three or more children indicated that their desire for a school near home was in part due to logistics: it was necessary that all the children could either walk or cycle to school and be independent when getting to after-school activities. Parents also indicated that they wanted their children to be at school with friends from the neighbourhood.

Parent F said that she would let her four children commute, but her preference was that they could cycle to a school near home. She articulated a view shared by many of the families when she concluded: 'I like that the school is near them because I want the kids that they go to school with to also live fairly close as well, so that they can hang out with them on the weekends. And I'm more likely to know who the kids are and know their families, you know, so that I can know where they are going and what they are up to. And I like to see them hopping on their bikes and going to school.'

While many parents present a strong argument for sending their children to schools near home, it is not always the best choice. If the school does not offer subjects that your child wants, or if your research suggests to you that your child wouldn't fit in, or be happy, then you may want to consider other options. If the local school is mixed and you have a strong preference for single-sex schools, then your child may have to travel further to get to one. If you want a school with a particular denominational tradition, particularly if you can only consider a school under the management of a 'minority' faith (e.g. Jewish, Muslim, Church of Ireland), then travel may be a necessity. In some cases, boarding school may also be an option.

What are the advantages of boarding school?

The number of boarding schools in Ireland has declined over the past twenty years and there are several reasons for this decline. Many boarding schools were owned and managed by Catholic teaching orders and the religious sisters, fathers and brothers in these orders played key roles in teaching and providing leadership and support. Because they lived within the community and on the school grounds, they provided constant supervision and care and did not expect to be paid for this. With the decline in numbers of persons entering religious orders, it became a financial impossibility to run many of these schools. It also brought about a change in the character of the schools, thereby making them very different from the communities which they once were.

Changes in Irish lifestyles also had consequences for boarding schools. For example, at a time when transportation was less developed and fewer families owned a car, it was often necessary to send children to a seven-day boarding school. There was also a time, before the introduction of free education in the late 1960s, when there were towns throughout the country with no secondary school.

Traditionally, boarding was sometimes favoured by families where both parents were involved in business or agricultural work. Boarding school, for such families, was not viewed as 'elite': it was an alternative to day schooling and was selected for practical reasons. Parents of large families also often favoured boarding schools. However, family size has decreased in Ireland and parents increasingly express interest in being closely involved in the upbringing of their children. Boarding schools were also favoured by parents who actively sought out schools with a distinct religious ethos. In an increasingly secular society, fewer parents demand such educational provision. As a consequence of all these changes, many boarding schools closed their doors.

Of the small number remaining, there are boarding schools within both the Catholic and Protestant traditions and there are single-sex and mixed boarding schools. Parents can choose between five-day and seven-day boarding in some of these schools. The fees for boarding schools vary somewhat and there are scholarship schemes and bursaries at schools that help defray costs. Appendix B at the back of this book indicates which schools offer boarding. Parents should contact the schools for information about facilities, fees and options such as five-day and seven-day boarding. Scholarships and grants should also be checked. For example, the Secondary Education Grants scheme makes provision for Protestant children attending schools under the management of the Church of Ireland.

There are also other factors to consider. Will your child like being away from home for part of the year? Will your child benefit from living with other young people? Will the study system be of support to your child? Is your child likely to enjoy the traditions associated with the school you have chosen (e.g. supporting rugby, cricket, choir), or might your child strongly dislike the activities that are central to the life of the school? It is important to give careful consideration to these questions when you are reading the literature sent to you by your selection of schools. It is also important to visit the schools and look at the dormitories, classrooms, recreation facilities and infirmary. Some boarding schools in Ireland are over-subscribed and may give preference to members of the church under whose management they operate (e.g. Church of Ireland/Catholic), or to siblings of pupils and to the children of past-pupils. Schools publish their admissions policy in their prospectus and/or on their websites.

Some of the families who were interviewed for this study had direct experience of boarding school education and were very positive about it. Parent B chose the boarding school he had attended for his son and his wife was supportive of the choice. However, she strongly favoured sending their daughter to a day school and did not consider sending her to a boarding school.

Parent R argued, in support of boarding schooling, that she believes it 'gives children a lot of freedom to become mature, in a very structured environment … and probably helps them become autonomous learners.' She selected a boarding school for her son, an only child, so that he would have a lot of company and structured activities with other boys after class every day. From her own experience of children who had attended boarding school, she argued that 'pupils at boarding school develop independence about things like looking after themselves and their clothes and equipment. They have to be organised, for study and for sports. And I think boarding school pupils often make profound and lasting friendships and have a strong sense of loyalty to their old school.'

Parent G had very different reasons for sending some of her children to boarding school. In a large family, far from needing company, the older children needed quiet in order to study. They also benefited from having their own space. By the time the younger 'half' of the family were teenagers, the older siblings had left home. There was plenty of space and less noise and interruption and thus there was no need to send the younger children to board, so they completed their education at local schools.

Many teachers and principals also support the view that boarding schools offer structure. One principal noted: 'One of the major advantages is the structure that is created. There is a fixed time for study every night; there is no alternative. There's no possibility of watching television, talking and texting on the mobile phone, or playing computer games. The only possibility is being in the study hall for the required three hours.'

Far from being exclusively suited to the academic child, this environment can sometimes support the kind of child who is likely to be easily distracted or a child who is unwilling to draw up a study timetable and stick to it. The principal pointed out: '... one of the difficulties for someone who has a problem with getting down to work, or with developing study habits, is the other options – listening to music, endless cups of coffee and so on. In the boarding situation, there simply are no options when it is study period.' This principal pointed out that the ordinary routines of family life are no longer completely forfeited by the boarding school pupil: 'Nowadays, a lot of children come home every single weekend because their schools have five-day boarding facilities. And even at seven-day boarding schools, they get home several times each term and they are home for mid-term breaks, long weekends and all the holidays. So they're not entirely divorced from family life from the age of twelve.'

The prospectuses of the boarding schools in this survey indicated that boarding schools in Ireland attempt to provide 'a homely, caring and secure environment' and also to 'inspire confidence and a mature independence' in pupils. Pupils are encouraged to develop a strong sense of team spirit, loyalty to each other and to their school. The 'house' system and the sporting traditions in many boarding schools encourage a kind of *esprit de corps*.

Different schools for siblings and moving your child to a different school

The needs and strengths of siblings vary and sometime parents find it best to send siblings to different second-level schools. In Ireland, the fact that there are still many single-sex schools means that sisters and brothers are often separated anyway. But there are instances when it is necessary to separate siblings even when it is easier for them to attend the same school. For example, if a younger child is likely to live very much in the shadow of older siblings who have distinguished themselves at a school, then a different school might be worth considering. If experience tells you that the school that your older children attend would not offer sufficient support for a younger child with special education needs, then it would be better to look around at other options rather than hoping that you can provide all the additional special needs support outside school. And if one of your children shows marked ability or interest in technical subjects, then it could be a mistake to send him or her to a school without those subjects, just because it served an older sibling very well.

Parents Q have seen their four children through school, university and on to successful careers. They chose a single-sex school for their son, 'who was bright but not a worker.' They were concerned that he was in danger of underachieving, considering his natural abilities. In the event, the teachers motivated him. As parent Q said: 'they sat on him and he has been studying ever since!' However, their daughter was neither motivated nor stimulated by the teaching at her single-sex school and they considered moving her from her school in fifth year. She resisted, as she did not want to leave her friends. Her parents agreed, but she had to develop self-motivation and independent study habits. She achieved her potential and, by staying, she also kept her valued friends. The decision not to move her proved to be the right one.

Sometimes parents keep siblings together, only to find out later that it would be best to move one of the children to a different school. Parents do not embark lightly on the job of moving a child to a different school – and often if a parent moves a child it is because the child has found it impossible to settle and do well in the school environment. Occasionally, parents move a child who has been bullied, even if the issue has been dealt with in full at school. In such a situation, parents might consider it best to give their child a 'fresh start' at a new school. Sometimes a move is encouraged by a school if the Principal and teachers are satisfied that the pupil cannot or will not co-operate with the staff and will not make any progress. Few parents move a child simply because the child demands it. Making a move is unsettling for the child and should be undertaken only after careful consideration of the options available.

Parent F commented that gossip and rumour sometimes cause parents to make hasty decisions about issues such as moving the child to another school. She said: '... parents make rash decisions and they move their children, you know, based on hearsay and issues that they might not have explored fully ... you hear [that] they moved them because there were awful stories ... I suppose I'm just perpetuating the parish pump thing, but my impression is that some people have moved their child because they heard that there was a poor teacher coming up and their child was going to get that teacher and they moved the child.' Rash decisions, made in reaction to rumour or pressures from an impulsive child, can be regretted deeply. If you are considering moving your child to a different school, be sure of the reasons why you/the school/the child want this move and be realistic about whether or not another school can really meet your requirements.

Summary

Just as it is important for parents to know something about the schools that they are considering for their child, it is equally important that parents 'know' the child for whom they are making decisions. Many parents say that they choose a school for their child on the basis of the school's 'reputation'. In relying on hearsay and grapevine knowledge, parents run the risk of hearing inaccurate or even conflicting descriptions of schools. However, parents view such local knowledge as important and as an inevitable part of the whole process of trying to select the right second-level school for their children. In some cases parents believe that the 'right' school will equip the pupil with academic skills and ensure good examination performance.

The parental emphasis on academic development and achievement is sometimes rooted in a belief that schools with an academic 'reputation' will somehow 'deliver' back to the parents a teenager with good Leaving Certificate results and good life prospects. Schools cannot and do not, make such promises. Firstly, schools do not measure their success in terms of examination results only, and, secondly, schools cannot transform every pupil into an academically strong young adult. Schools measure their success in other ways that, happily, are also important to many parents. They want pupils to have a balanced education and they are very aware of the role that schools play in forming the character of the young adult.

The 'character-forming' endeavours of many schools are evident in their commitment to supporting humanitarian and charitable foundations and through the development of traditions of support for school teams in areas such as sports and debating. Such activities often help uncover the strengths that really matter in adult life, such as empathy, diligence, loyalty, good humour and the ability to make and sustain real friendships.

6

Views from Schools

In researching this book, we contacted every second-level school, examined school literature, visited a number of schools and spoke with principals. In this chapter you can read the views of principals on issues such as discipline, school reputation, the happiness of the pupil and involving your child in choosing the school.

Which school is right?

Overwhelmingly, the teachers and principals we talked to considered that a good school is concerned with the holistic development of the student. It was recognised by principals that talking about 'holistic development' might seem like rhetoric, but even where they could see that the parents were more interested in examination preparation, the principals were clear that attention must be paid to the development of the whole child.

Principal B of a large community college argued that academic development could happen together with personal development: 'We have to look at what we're trying to achieve in the school, i.e. the complete development, the personal development, not only the academic development of the student. The argument sometimes is that you can't do both – I'm not inclined to agree with that.' In explaining what they meant by holistic development, principals referred frequently to the ways in which schools help young people to grow into 'good young people' and 'good citizens' who are 'well balanced.' They also referred to the aim, common to schools throughout Ireland, of developing the various 'talents' of their pupils and of instilling 'values' in pupils.

School information (such as the prospectus and the website) for most schools surveyed contains a statement about the values that the schools hope to transmit to their pupils. So, just as it is important to consider academic issues when trying to choose the 'right' school, it is also important to look at statements about values and ask yourself if these are particularly important to you and your family. Many schools express their values in terms such as 'a community which recognises the value and dignity of each person'; 'the encouragement of dignity and respect'; 'hard work and responsible behaviour'.

Some schools make it clear that their values have evolved from the education tradition to which the school belonged and an example would include fostering 'an understanding and critical appreciation of Christian values'. The statements about the values to which the school subscribes may appear under the heading of school ethos. Again, an ethos statement may refer to and have its roots in, the tradition of the school, or the religious order that founded the school.

For example, schools under the trusteeship of one of the orders of religious sisters express their commitment to 'an ethos which is firmly rooted in Christian principles. Each girl is encouraged to live her faith through prayer services, personal prayer, retreats and class masses.' By examining the value and/or ethos statements, you can get some insight into the spirit of the school and discuss this more fully with the principal. This is particularly important when the ethos statements refer to the religious observations of the school.

The prospectuses also outline aspects of academic relevance, such as facilities, curriculum, subjects available and commitment to academic endeavour. While most principals believed that schools were, firstly, about holistic development, they were pragmatic about parents' interest in academic performance. Principal B recognised that most parents measure this by how the pupils perform in public examinations and not by how the school has helped individual pupils to improve their academic achievement over time.

Indeed, some parents are only interested in public examination results and when they came to their first meeting with Principal B they would be 'unapologetic about looking for exam results'. Such parents are likely to believe that the reputation of the school is based on its academic success and they often have expectations about the academic performance of their own children.

Some school principals commented on parental expectations and on how schools are expected to meet all of these expectations. Principal D, also in a large community college (mixed), noted that 'the level of achievement [the parents] aspire to [for their child] is at least their own [level of achievement]. Parental aspiration is high.' Principal M, at a boys' secondary school, commented that 'certain parents would be very, very keyed into and be obsessed by the academic success ... they only focus on academic achievement.' However, despite the ever-increasing emphasis on achievement within the 'points' system, principals were emphatic that school has a role in areas additional to the academic.

Some schools provide sustained support to families in crisis so that their children can continue coming to school every day and experience some stability at a time of domestic difficulty. These schools are the 'right' school for their pupils precisely because the support and caring extend beyond anything that can be described in a prospectus or on a website, or measured in any kind of league table.

The reputation of the school

One of the principals with whom we spoke summed up the views of many other principals when she said that parents who are looking for the 'right' school are very influenced by the 'reputation' of a school: 'For those who want academic excellence, it's a reputation for academic achievement. For those who want discipline, it's that. For those who want their children to be happy, it's that. The parents talk to each other and find out about a school. Increasingly, the children decide for themselves and the parents let them take the decision. So, reputation, without a doubt, through the grapevine.'

Most parents become aware of the distinctive characteristics of a school because of the reputation that it has somehow developed. Principal X at a girls' secondary school concluded frankly that reputation nowadays is all about academic success: 'You can talk about the holistic education or the leadership offered by the principal, but what [parents] want first and foremost is good exam results – that's what they expect from us.'

Principal N, at a fee-paying secondary school (mixed), reflected on what he believed many parents looked for when they chose fee-paying schools: 'I think they choose a school that will give their children the right preparation for the profession they would like to see them enter, or the life they would like them to have. It's not just the academic, it's a life choice. Parents choose fee-paying schools for the results and also for the friends that their children will make, the networks they will create for the future. They are the two most important factors which influence parents in their choice of school.' In a similar vein, Principal T (community college, mixed) commented that 'some schools are chosen on status. We're in a very competitive environment here. Some parents will choose on the basis of the perceived status of a school even though it might not be the right one for their child. Parental expectations from a school are very high around here – they have ambition for their children and they expect a lot from the school.'

The dangers of choosing a school for perceived status were also pointed out by Principal Z (girls' fee-paying secondary school), who said that parents 'might choose a school for its prestige value. But whether it's the right school for their child only emerges as time goes on.' Despite her concern that parents might make choices based on 'prestige value', Principal Z nonetheless noted that many parents invest time and effort in trying to choose the right school: 'Some parents put a lot of hard work into choosing, but they can't really get the full picture until the child has been in the school for a while.' What they can do, she noted, is try to get a sense of the school from reliable informants such as past-pupils, or other parents who have sent children to the school under consideration.

Most of the principals agreed that people talk about the 'reputation' of schools and that a good reputation is built on having strengths in key areas such as discipline, academic development and good co-curricular activities. They also agreed that reputation is usually passed on the grapevine, a phenomenon discussed earlier in this book. Principal F (girls' secondary school), said that 'word of mouth' is hugely important in spreading information about a school. Principal J (girls' secondary school) agreed, saying that 'word of mouth is very important ... parents meet one another, at the primary school in particular and they ask about different schools and that is very important.' Discussion with both principals and parents in Ireland, therefore, confirmed the findings of some of the British research outlined in chapter two. It indicated that parents in Ireland use social networks and the grapevine to exchange information on schools – particularly information on schools that are perceived as academic.

The happiness of your child within a disciplined environment

The happiness of their pupils was referred to by most of the school principals who spoke with us and is also a feature of many school prospectuses. Principal B (community college) said that most parents took several factors into account when choosing a school, such as 'enthusiastic teaching', if these factors meant that their child would be happy at school. He commented that 'your ordinary middle-of-the-road parent [will be] looking at the happiness of the child and the child's involvement in everything in the school. When it comes to the crunch, parents will … accept a certain amount that isn't absolutely perfect.'

'Happiness is the big thing for parents', Principal F (girls' secondary school) told us. She commented that most parents are more concerned that their children settle and feel happy when they start second-level schooling, than they are about academic performance. Principal M (boys' secondary school) elaborated on this theme, giving perhaps the fullest summary: 'Every child should be happy coming to school. His unhappiness shouldn't be caused by a person – teacher or pupil – his unhappiness may be caused by a subject and we can't do much about that. We all hated something in our lives at school. But happiness should be the hallmark of the school. If a child is happy, he can function and develop. There is nothing I like more than when a parent says, 'My son was happy in your school.'

Many schools operate an 'open door' policy, to indicate clearly to parents that they are always welcome at the school and to demonstrate their commitment to maintaining a culture of care. In one girls' secondary school, Principal J explained that it was commonplace to meet parents around the school and they even had a Parents' Room, which was used by parents who participate in adult education classes. The Principal liked having parents on the school campus, even though it can be very demanding to operate an 'open door' policy. She described the easy relationship between parents and the school: 'They come and, very often, they've no appointment. Like today, now, a parent came and I had to say come back tomorrow because the Deputy was gone driving a group to a match and I had somebody else with me. I said, we'll ring you and we'll see you again. They come in for the smallest thing. Parents of academically-good and not so good. The tradition is in the school and I suppose … we're used to seeing parents around the school all day.' The Principal was confident that this kind of relationship with parents contributed to the overall 'caring atmosphere'. Like many principals, she believed that this atmosphere was of paramount importance in the school: 'If girls can go away saying there was a caring atmosphere, everybody was fairly treated [then] we witness gospel values in a real way. They are not just passing through – we really care about them.'

Caring for pupils invariably means providing discipline and structure and when parents select a school it is important that they become familiar with the code of conduct and the ways in which rule-breaking is treated. Most of the principals indicated that they had a structure based on keeping the lines of communication open. Notes sent home to parents and the inclusion of Year Heads in managing disciplinary issues were common features of discipline procedures. In some schools, discipline was particularly important as it was an expression of 'caring'. For example, in one boys' secondary school, Principal K commented that 'these kids need boundaries – they're not always getting that at home. A lot of our kids are living with grand-parents, or with their Mom half the week and Dad half the week, or every second week, so it's probably the minority that are living at home with Mom and Dad. All the more need for firm boundary management – and the pastoral role of teachers is crucial in a school like this. Teachers want to be aware if somebody has a serious problem; it influences the management of discipline and how we temper things. We give kids chances and we forgive them. You have to keep allowing them to come back.'

Moving schools and involving your child in the choice of school

You may be considering moving your child from one second-level school to another – perhaps at the request of the child. Parents are not always aware of the reasons that the child is pushing for a move to another school. It may be that most of their friends are at the preferred school, or it may be that the child has not settled at the second-level school originally chosen. Parents and teachers may want to ascertain whether or not the child has experienced bullying from classmates and is moving to get away from them.

Parents will also need to ascertain how much – and which parts – of the curriculum the pupil has covered in each subject before they make a move to another school. It is therefore strongly advised that parents communicate with the school and get a sense of why their child has suggested a move. One practical reason for this is that schools have different policies for accepting pupils in the middle of the school year or in the middle of a programme (the three-year junior cycle programme, or the two-year senior cycle programme).

These policies are worked out with a view to ensuring that incoming pupils make the transition to a new school with ease. In some cases, pupils have to join in the middle of the year if, for example, they have arrived from overseas. But in other cases it may be preferable to wait until the pupil has completed the programme. In one girls' secondary school, Principal J (girls' secondary school) and the Board of Management were of the view that pupils should ideally not join the school in the middle of a programme. She gave the example of a parent who had contacted her applying for a place for his daughter, who was in the middle of the second year of the junior cycle programme at another local school. The Principal explained that school policy was to request that the pupil waited to enter until after third year and therefore after she had done her Junior Certificate examination. The parent eventually agreed and the Principal commented that the pupil 'eventually moved after third year and she's very happy here now.'

Precisely why parents move their children to different local schools is not always clear and some schools never fully understand why a particular child has left. The same school principal continued to comment: 'I had two sisters, very good pupils, but the father was never happy and I wasn't sure why. Whatever we did wouldn't satisfy him, so he moved them both.' The inability to 'satisfy' every parent is something that schools deal with all the time.

Principal N (fee-paying mixed secondary school) made an observation echoed by other principals: 'After parents have chosen, they can have various reactions. Just as after any purchase you wonder afterwards if you have made the right decision, so it is with schools. They can reassure themselves that the decision is the right one by talking to other parents, confirming that the school is a good one, or they can start to doubt their decision … [This] can cause them to believe it is the wrong choice and then I find they become very bitter and react to everything very badly. They may decide to move the child because if they leave the child here they will continue to find fault with everything. That can happen and it is most unfortunate.'

Perhaps one reason that parents move their children to different schools in the middle of secondary education is that, according to many school principals, parents increasingly view education as a commodity. If they believe that they are not getting what they want at one school, they will look for another. 'Parents shop around', was an expression used by several principals with whom we spoke. Principal M (boys' secondary school) stated: 'There's a marketplace out there; people shop around and they ask questions. They're the customers.' Principal K (boys' secondary school) commented that he had witnessed a change in the criteria for choosing a school: 'When we were going to school, you went to a school because you had some family association there. I don't think it's tied like that anymore. I think people are more likely to travel if they have transport. They check out schools.'

Many parents now shop around, make a short list of their preferred schools and apply to all the schools on their list. Some submit applications several years before their child will be entering second-level education. They are willing to pay booking fees at a few schools if this is required, in order to have choices. Principals, therefore, have to be mindful of the fact that every applicant won't actually come to the school. In fact, one principal commented that parents apply 'who have no intention of sending their daughter' to the school, but they file an application as a 'fall-back' position in the event that they do not get their first or second choice of school in the area.

Making multiple applications may be perfectly sensible for parents, but can make planning difficult for principals. They often have to re-do their 'numbers' several times and send out late offers of first-year places to families during the summer. Nonetheless, they recognise that parents are looking for particular things from a school and are anxious to find what they believe is the 'right' school for their child. Principal M concluded: ' ... a lot of our pupils would pass some other schools on the way in here – equally, pupils would pass our school on the way to other schools – so choices are made ... it's good the parents have that choice.' For this reason many schools host an Open Day or Open Evening, when prospective pupils and their families may visit the school to talk with pupils and teachers and see the facilities. Principal K commented: 'We've had Open Nights and they've been really successful ... people were coming to look anyway and get a sense of the place even if they mightn't end up sending their child here.'

It is noteworthy that principals consider that increasingly 'the child has a say' about where they will go to school. Principal K believed that hosting the Open Night for prospective pupils contributed to that, as he observed that 'the child has a huge say [and] might decide to stay local, where his peer group is.' Principal M also commented on the fact that pupils are involved in the choice, but he was concerned that parents should not completely concede the ground to the child: ' ... a lot seem to leave it to the child and the child makes decisions [for reasons] that are very insignificant – the half-day on Wednesday, or the [fact that] the school has a swimming pool, rather than the academic or the holistic education.'

Summary

School principals concur with the view expressed in research literature that, increasingly, parents are shopping around and looking for the 'right' second-level school for their child. They can become confused with hearsay and grapevine knowledge and perceive one school as having more prestige or a better academic reputation than another school. Principals are supportive of the fact that parents look at several schools where possible, attend Open Days and information sessions and speak with past pupils. They recognise that the more informed parents are about schooling, the greater the possibility that they will make the right choice for their child. Information on the school ethos, its code of discipline and subject choice are listed in school literature. Parents should also visit the school. They will then be well equipped for the task of choosing the right school for their child.

Notes

1 D. Glendenning (1999), *Education and the Law* (Ireland: Butterworths), p. 27.

2 See A. Hyland and K. Milne (eds) (1992), *Irish Educational Documents* Vol. II, p. 467.

3 For a discussion of the impact of this policy, see Glendenning (1999), p. 32.

4 Glendenning (1999), p. 32.

5 J.Coolahan (1981), *Irish Education, History and Structure* (Dublin: IPA), p. 132.

6 Circular from the Minister for Education, George Colley, to the authorities of secondary and vocational schools, January 1966, p. 3, cited in Coolahan (1981), p. 194.

7 Cited in Hyland & Milne (1992), p. 267.

8 *Ibid.*, p. 268.

9 'Community School' (Memorandum of October, 1970), cited in Hyland & Milne (1992), p. 270.

10 B. Mooney, 'Career Guidance and Counselling' in B. Gilsenan (2004), *The Essential Parents' Guide to the Secondary School Years* (Dublin: Primary ABC), p. 12.

11 See for example J. Coldron and P. Boulton (1991), '"Happiness" as a criterion of parents' choice of school' in *Journal of Education Policy*, Vol. 6, No. 2; J.D. Willms & F. Echols (1992), 'Alert and Inert Clients: The Scottish Experience of Parental Choice of Schools' in *Economics of Education Review*, Vol. 2, No. 4; S.J. Ball (1993), 'Education Markets, Choice and Social Class: the market as a class strategy in the UK and the USA [1]', *British Journal of Sociology of Education*, Vol. 14, No. 1; P.A Woods (1996), 'Choice, class and effectiveness' in *School Effectiveness and School Improvement*, Vol. 7, No. 3; S.J. Ball & C. Vincent (1998), '"I heard it on the grapevine": "Hot" knowledge and school choice' in *British Journal of Sociology of Education*, Vol. 19, No. 3.

12 See Ball & Vincent (1998).

13 S.J. Ball, R. Bowe and S. Gewirtz (1996), 'School Choice, Social Class and Distinction: The Realisation of Social Advantage in Education' in *Journal of Education Policy*, Vol. 11, No. 1, p. 94.

14 *Ibid.*

15 S.J. Ball, R. Bowe and S. Gewirtz (1995), 'Circuits of Schooling: A sociological exploration of parental choice of school in social class contexts', *Sociological Review*, Vol. 43, No. 1,

pp. 66-7. See also D.T. Slaughter and B.L. Schneider (1986), *Newcomers: Blacks in Private Schools* (Evanston, Ill.: Northwestern University).

16 Ball, Bowe and Gewirtz (1995), p. 57.

17 *Ibid.*, p.63.

18 *Ibid.*

19 Willms & Echols (1992), p. 341.

20 Ball, Bowe and Gewirtz (1995), p. 71.

21 See J. Maddaus (1990), 'Parental Choice of School: What Parents Think and Do', *Review of Research in Education*, 16, C.B Cazden (ed.), (Washington, DC: AERA); Slaughter & Schneider (1986).

22 A. West (1994), 'Choosing a School – The Consumer's Perspective' in M.J. Halstead (ed.), *Parental Choice and Education: Principles, Policy and Practice* (London: Kogan Page), pp. 113-15.

23 Ball and Vincent (1998), p. 378.

24 *Ibid.*, p. 381.

25 *Ibid.*

26 Parental interview cited in Ball & Vincent (1998), p. 385.

27 M.David, A. West and J. Ribbens (1994), *Mother's Intuition* (London: Falmer Press), p. 53.

28 D. Reay (1998), 'Engendering Social Reproduction: mothers in the educational marketplace', *British Journal of Sociology of Education*, Vol. 19, No. 2, p. 200.

29 For a discussion of 'hot' knowledge and the grapevine see Ball & Vincent (1998), p. 380.

30 Ball & Vincent (1998), p. 389.

31 E. Smyth (1999), *Do Schools Differ? Academic and Personal Development among Pupils in the Second-Level Sector* (Dublin: ESRI General Research Series, Oak Tree Press), p. 50.

32 *Ibid.*, p. 11.

33 *Ibid.*, p. 213.

34 *Ibid.*, p. 213-14.

35 See K. Lynch (1999), *Equality in Education* (Dublin: Gill and Macmillan), pp. 271-72.

36 S. Drudy and K. Lynch (1993), *Schools and Society in Ireland* (Dublin: Gill and Macmillan), p. 246.

37 See D. Hannan and M. Boyle (1987), *Schooling Decisions: the Origins and Consequences of Selection and Streaming in Irish Post-Primary Schools* (Dublin: ESRI).

38 Drudy and Lynch, p. 247.

39 Smyth (1999), p. 186.

40 *Ibid.*, p. 55.

41 *Ibid.*

42 *Ibid.*, p. 224.

43 *Ibid.*, p. 53.

44 *Ibid.*, p. 218-19.

45 See R. Breen and D. Hannan (1987), 'School and Gender: The Education of Girls in Ireland' in *Gender in Irish Society*, C. Curtin, P. Jackson, B. O'Connor (eds), (Galway: GUP).

46 M. Brennan (1986) 'Factors Affecting Attainment in the Irish Leaving Certificate Examination' (unpublished M.Ed. thesis, University College Dublin), cited in Drudy & Lynch (1993), p. 197.

47 *Ibid.*

48 Drudy & Lynch (1993), p. 197, citing Hannan *et al* (1983), *Schooling and Sex Roles: Sex Differences in Subject Provision and Student Choice in Irish Post-Primary Schools* (Dublin: ESRI General Research Series, Oak Tree Press).

49 J. Elwood and K. Carlisle (2003), *Examining Gender, Gender and Achievement in the Junior and Leaving Certificate Examinations 2000/2001* (Dublin: NCCA).

50 *Ibid.*, p. 104.

51 See D. Hannan, *et al* (1996), *Coeducation and Gender Equality: Exam Performance, Stress and Personal Development* (Ireland: ESRI General Research Series, Oak Tree Press) and also E. Smyth (1999).

52 Drudy & Lynch (1993), p. 198.

53 *Ibid.*, p. 183, citing K. Lynch (1989), *The Hidden Curriculum: Reproduction in Education, A Reappraisal* (Lewes: Falmer Press).

54 Smyth (1999), p. 106.

55 C. Itzin (1985), *How to choose a school* (London: Methuen), p. 179.

Bibliography

Official Publications

Irish Education Inquiry, First Report HC 1825 (400, xii, p. 255).

The Intermediate Education (Ireland) Act, 1878.

The Agriculture and Technical Instruction (Ireland) Act, 1899.

The Intermediate Education (Amendment) Act, 1924.

The School Attendance Act, 1926.

The Vocational Education Act, 1930.

Report of the Commission of Inquiry on Mental Handicap, 1965.

Circular from the Minister for Education, George Colley, to the authorities of secondary and vocational schools, January 1966.

The Vocational Education (Amendment) Act, 1970.

The Education Act, 1998.

The Education (Welfare) Act, 2000.

Education for Persons with Special Educational Needs Act, 2004.

State Examinations Commission Annual Report, 2004.

Books

Adler, M. et al, *Parental Choice and Educational Policy* (Edinburgh: Edinburgh University Press, 1989).

Akenson, D., *The Irish Education Experiment* (London: Routledge & Kegan Paul, 1970).

Ball, S. J., *The Micropolitics of the School* (London: Methuen, 1987).

Bernstein, B., *Class, Codes and Control*, Vol. 3 (London: Routledge, 1975).

Coolahan, J., *Irish Education, History and Structure* (Dublin: IPA, 1981; 1983).

Curtin, C. *et al.* (eds), *Gender in Irish Society* (Galway: GUP, 1987).

David, M. *et al.*, *Mother's Intuition? Choosing Secondary Schools* (London: Falmer Press, 1994).

Drudy, S. and K. Lynch, *Schools and Society in Ireland* (Dublin: Gill and Macmillan, 1993).

Drudy, S. and M. Uí Chatháin, *Gender Equality in Classroom Interaction* (Maynooth: NUIM, 1999).

Elwood, J. and K. Carlisle, *Examining Gender, Gender and Achievement in the Junior and Leaving Certificate Examinations* (Dublin: NCCA, 2003).

Glendenning, D., *Education and the Law* (Ireland: Butterworths, 1999).

Halstead, M. J. (ed.), *Parental Choice and Education: Principles, Policy and Practice* (London: Kogan Page, 1994).

Hannan, D. *et al.*, *Schooling and Sex Roles: Sex Differences in Subject Provision and Student Choice in Irish Post-Primary Schools* (Dublin: ESRI General Research Series, Oak Tree Press, 1983).

Hannan, D. *et al.*, *Coeducation and Gender Equality: Exam Performance, Stress and Personal Development* (Ireland: ESRI General Research Series, Oak Tree Press, 1996).

Hyland, A. and K. Milne (eds), *Irish Educational Documents*, Vol. I. (Dublin: CICE, 1987).

_____ *Irish Educational Documents*, Vol. II. (Dublin: CICE, *1992).

Itzin, C., *How to Choose a School* (London: Methuen, 1985).

Lynch, K., *The Hidden Curriculum: Reproduction in Education, A Reappraisal* (Lewes: Falmer Press, 1989).

Lynch, K., *Equality in Education* (Dublin: Gill and Macmillan, 1999).

Slaughter, D.T. and B.L. Schneider, *Newcomers: Blacks in Private Schools* (Evanston, Ill.: Northwestern University, 1986).

Smyth, E., *Do Schools Differ? Academic and Personal Development among Pupils in the Second-Level Sector* (Dublin: ESRI General Research Series, Oak Tree Press, 1999).

Wellman, B. and S. Berkowitz (eds), *Social Structures: a network approach* (Cambridge: CUP, 1988).

Woods, P. *et al.*, *School Choice and Competition: Markets in the Public Interest?* (London and New York: Routledge, 1998).

Articles

Ball, S.J. 'Education Markets, Choice and Social Class: the market as a class strategy in the UK and the USA [1]' in *British Journal of Sociology of Education*, Vol. 14, No. 1, 1993.

Ball, S.J. *et al.*, 'Circuits of schooling: A Sociological exploration of parental choice of school in social class contexts' in *Sociological Review,* Vol. 43, No. 1, 1995.

Ball, S.J. *et al.*, 'School choice, social class and distinction: the realization of social advantage in education' in *Journal of Education Policy,* Vol. 11, No. 1, 1996.

Ball, S.J. and C. Vincent, ' "I heard it on the grapevine": "hot" knowledge and school choice' in *British Journal of Sociology of Education,* Vol. 19, No. 3, 1998.

Blank, R., 'Educational Effects of Magnet High Schools', in Clune, W. and J. Witte (eds), Choice and Control in *American Education,* Vol. 3 (Lewes: Falmer Press, 1990).

Breen, R. and D. Hannan, 'School and Gender: The Education of Girls in Ireland' in Curtin, C. *et al.*, *Gender in Irish Society* (Galway: GUP, 1987).

Coldron, J. and P. Boulton, ' "Happiness" as a criterion of parents' choice of school' in *Journal of Education Policy,* Vol. 6, No. 2, 1991.

Eccles, F. *et al.*, 'Parental Choice in Scotland', in *Journal of Education Policy,* Vol. 5, No. 3, 1990.

Maddaus, J., 'Parental Choice of School: What Parents Think and Do' in *Review of Research in Education, 16* (ed.) C.B. Cazden (Washington DC: AERA, 1990).

Moore, D., 'Voice and Choice in Chicago', in *Clune, W. and J. Witte* (eds), *Choice and Control in American Education,* Vol. 3 (Lewes: Falmer Press, 1990).

Reay, D., 'Engendering Social Reproduction: mothers in the educational marketplace' in *British Journal of Sociology of Education,* Vol. 19, No. 2, 1998.

Wellman, B. *et al.*, 'Networks as personal communities' in Wellman, B. and S. Berkowitz (eds) *Social Structures: a network approach* (Cambridge: CUP, 1988).

West, A., 'Factors affecting choice of school for middle class parents: implications for marketing' in *Educational Management and Administration,* Vol. 20, No. 4, 1992.

West, A., 'Choosing a School - The Consumer's Perspective' in *Halstead, M.J.* (ed.), *Parental Choice and Education: Principles, Policy and Practice* (London: Kogan Page, 1994).

West, A. and A. Varlaam, 'Choice of secondary school: parents of junior school children', in *Educational Research,* Vol. 33, No. 1, 1991.

Willms, J.D. and F. Echols, 'Alert and Inert Clients: the Scottish Experience of Parental Choice of Schools' in *Economics of Education Review,* Vol. 2, No. 4, 1992.

Woods, P.A., 'Changing schools?' in *Management in Education,* Vol. 6, No. 1, 1992.

_____ 'Choice, class and effectiveness' in *School Effectiveness and School Improvement,* Vol. 7, No. 3, 1996.

Unpublished dissertations and theses

Brennan, M., 'Factors Affecting Attainment in the Irish Leaving Certificate Examination' (unpublished M.Ed. thesis, University College Dublin, 1986).

Websites

www.education.ie   Department of Education and Science
www.educonsult.ie   Education Consultants
www.edunet.ie/parents   National Parents Council Post-Primary
www.examinations.ie   State Examinations Commission
www.ncca.ie   National Council for Curriculum and Assessment
www.qualifax.ie   Jointly produced by the Institute of Guidance Counsellors and the Department of Education and Science

Appendix A

Programmes and Examinations

The factual information in this appendix is taken from the published literature of the National Council for Curriculum and Assessment (NCCA), from their website *www.ncca.ie* and from the Department of Education and Science (DES) website *www.education.ie*

The authors gratefully acknowledge the cooperation of the NCCA, the DES and the State Examinations Commission (SEC).

Junior Cycle

The Junior Cycle covers the first three years of second-level schooling which are also the last three years of compulsory schooling (see Fig. A.1).

Fig. A.1 Junior Cycle

Programme	Junior Cycle
Duration	3 years
Public examination	Junior Certificate

At the end of the three years, pupils sit the Junior Certificate Examination. (An alternative to this examined programme is the Junior Certificate School Programme.) The programme has been designed to ensure that those for whom it represents the end of formal education will have been exposed to a wide range of educational experience which will help them to prepare for life after school, while those who remain in the school system will have been offered a sufficiently broad base from which to select subject areas for senior cycle. The junior cycle programme builds on the educational foundation which has been laid down in primary school. However, it also represents a substantial advance on that educational experience in terms of depth, range and quality. So, for instance, it is intended to help the pupil not just to acquire more knowledge and to solve more problems, but also to develop socially and personally, morally and spiritually. In this regard, it specifically addresses issues in the areas of social, personal and health education, as well as civic, environmental and political responsibility. 'The programme is intended to prepare the young person for the responsibilities of citizenship in the national context and in the context of the wider European and global communities.' (Source: *www.ncca.ie*)

For convenience and clarity, we list below the broad areas of experience which the NCCA has prescribed for junior cycle, with the corresponding subjects.

Fig. A.2 Junior Cycle Curriculum

Areas of Experience	Subjects include
Language, Literature and Communication	Irish; English; Classical Studies; Latin; Greek; French; German; Italian; Spanish
Mathematical Studies and Applications	Mathematics
Science and Technology	Science; Materials Technology Wood; Metalwork; Technology; Technical Graphics
Social, Political and Environmental Education	Civic, Social and Political Education (CSPE); Environmental and Social Studies; Business Studies; Geography; History; Home Economics; Social, Personal and Health Education (SPHE)
Arts Education	Art, Craft, Design; Music
Physical Education	PE, individual and team sports
Religious and Moral Education	RE
Guidance, Counselling and Pastoral Care	Services offered by the school

Data source: www.ncca.ie

The Junior Certificate School Programme (JCSP) is available as an alternative. It has been designed to meet the needs of particular groups of pupils. For instance, some young people who are not academically inclined could leave school at sixteen years of age with no qualification, if the only programme on offer to them is an academic one. This programme, on the other hand, can be used by their teachers to present information in a way which suits their needs and taps into their interests. This encourages them to respond in a positive way and to experience success. It is currently offered in about 150 schools throughout the country.

At the end of the three-year programme, pupils receive a 'profile' which is an official record of their achievements, validated by the Department of Education and Science. The profile consists of over one hundred 'statements'. There are two types of statements: subject-based statements and cross-curricular statements. Subject-based statements are closely related to the Junior Certificate syllabus subjects. Cross-curricular statements allow students to make practical connections between the different subjects. For example, they might demonstrate their mathematical skills by measuring in woodwork class, or design a menu in art class for use in home economics. They are awarded certification for a wide range of achievements, such as punctuality or the ability to work in groups.

Junior Certificate Examination

The State Examinations Commission has statutory responsibility for matters relating to all public examinations. All examinations take place nationally in June and all are externally marked.

The Junior Certificate Examination is the final examination for the junior cycle. Papers may be taken at higher or ordinary level and, in the case of English, Irish and mathematics, a foundation level is also available. There are core subjects which include Irish; English; mathematics; Social Personal & Health Education (SPHE); Civic, Social and Political Education (CSPE); and two other subjects from a list which includes languages, science, business studies, art, music, religion, history and geography. Most pupils sit nine or ten subjects in this examination. The Junior Certificate subjects are shown in Fig. A.3, listed below:

Fig. A.3 Junior Certificate Subjects

Art, Craft, Design	Latin
Business Studies	Materials Technology (Wood)
Civic, Social and Political Education	Mathematics
Classical Studies	Metalwork
English	Music
Environmental and Social Studies	Physical Education (non-exam)
French	Religious Education
Gaeilge (Irish)	Science
Geography	Social, Personal and Health Education (non-exam)
German	Spanish
Greek	Technical Graphics
History	Technology
Home Economics	Typewriting
Italian	

Data source: www.education.ie

Senior Cycle

Transition Year

In fourth year, most second-level schools offer pupils a Transition Year Programme. In some schools this is built into a six-year secondary cycle, balancing three years in the junior cycle with three years in the senior cycle. In others it is an option, with some students choosing to take it and others choosing to enter the two-year senior cycle directly after their Junior Certificate examination (see Fig. A.4).

Fig. A.4 Senior Cycle

Programme	Senior Cycle
Duration	2 or 3 years
Public examination	Leaving Certificate

The idea behind Transition Year is to break away from what is perceived by some as a subject-led, examination-driven system into a more interdisciplinary, student-centred year. For most pupils, it provides a welcome opportunity to explore areas of educational experience in a non-examination environment. In this way it represents a 'year out' following the Junior Certificate examination and before embarking on the Leaving Certificate programme.

It can happen that pupils are so intent on passing their examinations that they lose sight of the richness and variety inherent in a broad educational experience. Transition Year, by giving them breathing space, can help them to appreciate the wider aspects of education and to take responsibility for their own learning ('self-directed' learning).

Transition Year has three main aims:
- Education for maturity with an emphasis on personal development, including social awareness and increased social competence
- The promotion of general, technical and academic skills with an emphasis on interdisciplinary and self-directed learning
- Education through experience of adult and working life as a basis for personal development and maturity.

Data source: www.ncca.ie

The main difference between this year and the other five at second level is that each school has the freedom to design its own programme, within set guidelines, which can be unique to that school and can respond both to the student population and to the environment in which the school is situated. In all other years, schools follow the syllabus laid down by the Department of Education and Science and on which their pupils are examined in the two public examinations. In Transition Year, therefore, the scope to innovate and explore is very much greater. In some schools, the Parents' Association and the Student Council are quite involved in aspects of the year. Some schools organize work experience, so that their Transition Year pupils can experience career areas that interest them. This often helps them to make a more informed choice of career. More immediately, the range of education experience often opens their eyes to subject areas they might not have considered before Transition Year.

Fifth and Sixth Year

When they progress into fifth year, most senior cycle pupils choose the established **Leaving Certificate** programme. They will have made subject choices during their third or fourth year, which will involve leaving some subjects behind. All pupils are required to study Irish (unless exempted for reasons which might include, for instance, their place of birth); most also study English and mathematics. After that, there is a wide range of subjects to choose from. Clearly, not all schools will offer all subjects. Indeed, if they did, the choice would be far too wide. Most pupils take seven subjects in these two years. Depending on their particular abilities and ambitions, they may take two languages, or two science subjects. If they do that, there are then just two more subjects to choose from a wide array which includes history, geography, accounting, business, art, music, home economics and more.

The **Leaving Certificate Vocational Programme (LCVP)** is designed to give pupils the Leaving Certificate experience with some added dimensions of a kind similar to those offered by Transition Year. In other words, this two-year programme combines the academic strengths of the established Leaving Certificate with other elements such as work experience, self-directed learning and enterprise. Pupils learn through experience to work with others as part of a team and to explore various career options. Clear expression and effective communication are key competencies and students are encouraged to develop their skills in the use of information and communication technologies.

LCVP is a two-year programme made up as follows:

- At least five Leaving Certificate subjects one of which must be Irish and two selected from Vocational Subject Groupings. The subjects in the Vocational Subject Groupings include Construction Studies; Engineering; Agricultural Science; Physics; Chemistry; Biology; Home Economics; Art; Music.

Two additional courses of study, known as the Link Modules:

• These are: Preparation for the World of Work and Enterprise Education. In the Preparation for the World of Work module, pupils investigate local business and industry for employment opportunities; develop job-seeking skills and gain valuable practical experience of the world of work including shadowing a person in a career area that interests them. The Enterprise module helps pupils to become involved in organising visits to local business and community enterprises; meet and interview enterprising people on-site and in the classroom; plan and undertake interesting activities that will build self-confidence and creativity and develop teamwork, communication and computer skills.

Data source: www.ncca.ie

As an alternative to those two programmes, there is the **Leaving Certificate Applied** which is also a self-contained two-year programme. This programme is ideal for those whose plan is to go straight from school into employment. The focus in fifth and sixth years for those taking the established Leaving Certificate or the LCVP is inclined to be on the achievement of 'points' in order to progress to third-level education. That can alienate the significant minority whose life plan is different. This programme is designed to make their experience of the final two years in education meaningful and fulfilling. It allows them to experience success in terms of certification when they leave school. The programme involves active learning and practical tasks that engage the students. The main aim is to prepare them for transition to the world of work. First and foremost, it tries to ensure that their literacy and numeracy skills are developed to their full potential, but also that the pupils themselves develop personally and socially. To this end, they are given opportunities to undertake tasks outside the immediate school environment and to reflect on their achievement.

The continuous assessment offers great encouragement and an incentive to keep working throughout the programme. The two-year horizon of the established Leaving Certificate is simply too far away for many pupils; this programme brings assessment and feedback closer. It also means that the build-up and consequent stress involved in working towards one final examination is greatly reduced, as the LCA assessment breaks down into two-thirds continuous assessment; one-third terminal examination. It is ideal for pupils who may have difficulty with one final examination, which involves memorising, on the one hand and lengthy writing, on the other. The Leaving Certificate Applied programme also provides access to further education and training.

The LCA is made up of a range of courses that are structured round three elements:

- Vocational preparation
- Vocational education
- General education.

Courses are designed on a modular basis and are of thirty hours duration. Each year is divided into two sessions (September to January and February to May).

Learners must take a total of 44 modules. They are also required to complete seven Student Tasks over the two years.

Data source: www.ncca.ie

Student tasks range over contemporary issues (a project on drugs or poverty, for instance), practical issues such as completing a physical piece of work (a table, a sculpture) and also skills such as driving.

Certification in the Leaving Certificate Applied will not qualify these students for direct entry to third level courses, as that is not its intention. However, it does not cut off the possibility of further study, as those who successfully complete the programme will be able to proceed to many Post-Leaving Certificate courses.

Leaving Certificate Examination

At the end of senior cycle, pupils who have followed the established Leaving Certificate and the Leaving Certificate Vocational Programme take the Leaving Certificate Examination. Papers can be taken at higher or ordinary level (with an additional foundation level in mathematics).

The subjects currently available for examination are listed in alphabetical order in Fig. A.5, listed below:

Fig. A.5 Leaving Certificate Subjects

Accounting	Economics	Japanese
Agricultural Economics	Engineering	Mathematics
Agricultural Science	English	Music
Applied Maths	French	Physics
Arabic	Gaeilge (Irish)	Physics and Chemistry
Art		
Biology	Geography	Religious Education
Business	German	Russian
Chemistry	Graphics	Spanish
Classical Studies	History	Technical Drawing
Construction Studies	Home Economics	Technology
Design & Communication	Italian	

Data source: www.education.ie

Achievement in this examination is directly linked to processes of selection for courses of study in further and higher education. Normally, pupils sit seven subjects in this examination. The results of six of these are taken into account to decide their level of 'points' for the purposes of entry to third level-education (see Chapter One).

Pupils who opt for the Leaving Certificate Vocational Programme (LCVP) follow the same subject syllabuses and are assessed in the same way as their peers in the established Leaving Certificate by final examination in June. Their two Link Modules are examined in May and assessed as a unit. Assessment, which is at a common level, comprises two elements: an examination paper (40%) and a portfolio of course work (60%). Pupils are awarded a distinction, merit or pass grade in their Link Modules. These grades may be reckonable for entry into higher education. Their Leaving Certificate examination results are, of course, reckonable in the same way as they are for the established Leaving Certificate candidates.

As indicated above, Leaving Certificate Applied (LCA) pupils collect credits as they complete their course work through continuous assessment. It is possible to collect a total of 200 credits. In addition, they are required to undertake seven Tasks over the two years of the programme. The final examinations take place at the same time as the traditional Leaving Certificate. However, since 66% of the overall marks are available for satisfactory completion of the Modules and Tasks prior to the terminal examinations, just one-third of their marks comes from this examination. Awards are made at the distinction merit and pass levels.

Appendix B

Compiled from the Department of Education and Science data. The authors would like to thank the DES for their assistance.

Details are correct as of the time of publication.

Borris Vocational School

Address	Borris, Co. Carlow
Telephone	059-9773155
Email	bvsoffice@eircom.net
Principal	Breda Nolan
School Type	Vocational; Day
Enrolment	240 boys; 223 girls
Denomination	Interdenominational
Fees	No

Carlow Vocational School

Address	Kilkenny Road, Carlow Town
Telephone	059-9131187
Email	info@carlowife.ie
Principal	Bernard Mulchrone
School Type	Vocational; Day
Enrolment	310 boys; 598 girls
Denomination	Interdenominational
Fees	No

Presentation College

Address	Askea, Carlow, Co. Carlow
Telephone	059-9143927
Email	info@presentationcollegecarlow.com
Principal	Sean Mulvihill
School Type	Secondary; Day
Enrolment	295 boys; 307 girls
Denomination	Roman Catholic
Fees	No

St Leo's College

Address	Convent of Mercy, Dublin Road, Carlow Town
Telephone	059-9143660
Email	stleos@iol.ie
Principal	Clare Ryan
School Type	Secondary; Day
Enrolment	835 girls
Denomination	Roman Catholic
Fees	No

St Mary's Academy CBS

Address	Station Road, Carlow
Telephone	059-9142419
Email	principal@cbscarlow.net
Principal	Leo Hogan
School Type	Secondary; Day
Enrolment	457 boys
Denomination	Roman Catholic
Fees	No

Gaelcholáiste Cheatharlach

Address	Easca, Ceatharlach
Telephone	059-9132130
Email	gccoifig@eircom.net
Principal	Caitlín Mhic Cárthaigh
School Type	Vocational; Day; All tuition through Irish
Enrolment	122 boys; 99 girls
Denomination	Interdenominational
Fees	No

Coláiste Eoin

Address	Hacketstown, Co. Carlow
Telephone	059-6471198
Email	ceoifig@eircom.net
Principal	Michael Daly
School Type	Vocational; Day; All tuition through Irish
Enrolment	127 boys; 140 girls
Denomination	Interdenominational
Fees	No

St Mary's Knockbeg College

Address	Knockbeg, Co. Carlow
Telephone	059-9142127
Email	knockbegcollege@eircom.net
Principal	Cyril Hughes
School Type	Secondary; Day & Boarding
Enrolment	335 boys
Denomination	Roman Catholic
Fees	Day No Boarding Yes

Vocational School Muine Bheag

Address	Muine Bheag, Co. Carlow
Telephone	059-9721335
Email	muinebheagvs@eircom.net
Principal	Edmund Burke
School Type	Vocational; Day
Enrolment	97 boys; 182 girls
Denomination	Interdenominational
Fees	No

Presentation/De La Salle College

Address	Royal Oak Road, Muine Bheag, Co. Carlow
Telephone	059-9721860
Email	pdlsb@eircom.net
Principal	Anne Keating
School Type	Secondary; Day
Enrolment	220 boys; 198 girls
Denomination	Roman Catholic
Fees	No

Tullow Community School

Address	The Mullawn, Tullow, Co. Carlow
Telephone	059-9151473
Email	tulcomcw@iol.ie
Principal	Christopher McQuinn
School Type	Community; Day
Enrolment	299 boys; 387 girls
Denomination	Interdenominational
Fees	No

Bailieborough Community School

Address	Bailieborough, Co. Cavan
Telephone	042-9665295
Email	bailieborocs@eircom.net
Principal	Valerie McCormick
School Type	Community; Day
Enrolment	280 boys; 253 girls
Denomination	Interdenominational
Fees	No

St Clare's College

Address	Virginia Road, Ballyjamesduff, Co. Cavan
Telephone	049-8544551
Email	stclares@eircom.net
Principal	Sean Fegan
School Type	Secondary; Day
Enrolment	124 boys; 138 girls
Denomination	Roman Catholic
Fees	No

St Bricin's Vocational School

Address	Belturbet, Co. Cavan
Telephone	049-9522170
Email	bricin@iol.ie
Principal	John Gildea
School Type	Vocational; Day
Enrolment	78 boys; 84 girls
Denomination	Interdenominational
Fees	No

CO. CAVAN

St Mogue's College

Address	Bawnboy, Belturbet, Co. Cavan
Telephone	049-9523112
Email	mogues@iol.ie
Principal	James McGuinn
School Type	Vocational; Day
Enrolment	41 boys; 119 girls
Denomination	Interdenominational
Fees	No

Cavan Vocational School

Address	Cootehill Road, Cavan, Co. Cavan
Telephone	049-4331735
Email	cvs2003@eircom.net
Principal	John Kearney
School Type	Vocational; Day
Enrolment	240 boys; 206 girls
Denomination	Interdenominational
Fees	No

Loreto College

Address	Cavan, Co. Cavan
Telephone	049-4332881
Email	office@loretocavan.ie
Principal	Margaret Donagh
School Type	Secondary; Day
Enrolment	662 girls
Denomination	Roman Catholic
Fees	No

Royal School Cavan

Address	College Street, Cavan, Co. Cavan
Telephone	049-4361605
Email	royalschoolcavan@iol.ie
Principal	Ivan W Bolton
School Type	Secondary; Day & Boarding
Enrolment	87 boys; 109 girls
Denomination	Church of Ireland
Fees	Day Yes Boarding Yes

St Patrick's College

Address	Cavan, Co. Cavan
Telephone	049-4361888
Email	principal@stpatscavan.com
Principal	Dr Liam McNiffe
School Type	Secondary; Day
Enrolment	532 boys
Denomination	Roman Catholic
Fees	No

St Aidan's Comprehensive School

Address	Cootehill, Co. Cavan
Telephone	049-5552161
Email	staidansoffice@eircom.net
Principal	Anne Marie Lacey
School Type	Comprehensive; Day
Enrolment	258 boys; 267 girls
Denomination	Interdenominational
Fees	No

Virginia Vocational School

Address	Virginia, Co. Cavan
Telephone	049-8547050
Email	vvsoffice@eircom.net
Principal	Desmond Mooney
School Type	Vocational; Day
Enrolment	284 boys; 236 girls
Denomination	Interdenominational
Fees	No

Coláiste Mhuire

Address	Harmony Row, Ennis, Co. Clare
Telephone	065-6829497
Email	cmennis@eircom.net
Principal	Jean Pound
School Type	Secondary; Day
Enrolment	609 girls
Denomination	Roman Catholic
Fees	No

CO. CLARE

Ennis Community College

Address	Ennis, Co. Clare
Telephone	065-6829432
Email	ecc@ecc.ennis.tinet.ie
Principal	Matt Power
School Type	Vocational; Day; One stream has all tuition through Irish
Enrolment	172 boys; 222 girls
Denomination	Interdenominational
Fees	No

Rice College

Address	New Road, Ennis, Co. Clare
Telephone	065-6822105
Email	ricecollegecbs@eircom.net
Principal	Thomas Clohessy
School Type	Secondary; Day
Enrolment	334 boys; 253 girls
Denomination	Roman Catholic
Fees	No

St Flannan's College

Address	Ennis, Co. Clare
Telephone	065-6828019
Email	stflannans@eircom.net
Principal	Colm McDonagh
School Type	Secondary; Day & Boarding
Enrolment	786 boys; 264 girls
Denomination	Roman Catholic
Fees	Day No Boarding Yes

Ennistymon Vocational School

Address	Ennistymon, Ennis, Co. Clare
Telephone	065-7071375
Email	entvoc.ias@eircom.net
Principal	Enda Byrt
School Type	Vocational; Day
Enrolment	82 boys; 19 girls
Denomination	Interdenominational
Fees	No

Meánscoil na mBráithre

Address	Ennistymon, Co. Clare
Telephone	065-7071349
Email	cbsennistymon@eircom.net
Principal	Michael Concannon
School Type	Secondary; Day
Enrolment	208 boys
Denomination	Roman Catholic
Fees	No

Scoil Mhuire

Address	Ennistymon, Co. Clare
Telephone	065-7071224
Email	staffmail.ias@eircom.net
Principal	Seosamhín Uí Dhomhnallain
School Type	Secondary; Day
Enrolment	301 girls
Denomination	Roman Catholic
Fees	No

St John Bosco Community College

Address	Cahercon, Kildysart, Co. Clare
Telephone	065-6832300
Email	cahercon.ias@eircom.net
Principal	Marion Coughlan-Flynn
School Type	Vocational; Day
Enrolment	113 boys; 119 girls
Denomination	Interdenominational
Fees	No

St Joseph's Community College

Address	Carrigaholt Road, Kilkee, Co. Clare
Telephone	065-9056446
Email	kkeecomcoll.ias@eircom.net
Principal	Sylvester Barrett
School Type	Vocational; Day
Enrolment	124 boys; 159 girls
Denomination	Interdenominational
Fees	No

St Anne's Community College

Address	Killaloe, Co. Clare
Telephone	061-376257
Email	killaloecc@tinet.ie
Principal	John Fitzgibbon
School Type	Vocational; Day
Enrolment	171 boys; 188 girls
Denomination	Interdenominational
Fees	No

St Michael's Community College

Address	Kilmihil, Co. Clare
Telephone	065-9050021
Email	stmichaels@kilmihilcc.com
Principal	Helena Keane
School Type	Vocational; Day
Enrolment	164 boys; 152 girls
Denomination	Interdenominational
Fees	No

Kilrush Community School

Address	Kilrush, Co. Clare
Telephone	065-9051359
Email	administrator@kilrushcoms.com
Principal	Rock Kirwin
School Type	Community; Day
Enrolment	160 boys; 192 girls
Denomination	Interdenominational
Fees	No

Mary Immaculate Secondary School

Address	Lisdoonvarna, Co. Clare
Telephone	065-7074266
Email	lisdoon@iol.ie
Principal	John O'Loughlin
School Type	Secondary; Day
Enrolment	121 boys; 155 girls
Denomination	Roman Catholic
Fees	No

St Joseph's Secondary School

Address	Spanish Point, Milltown Malbay, Co. Clare
Telephone	065-7084311
Email	spoint@iol.ie
Principal	Mary Crawford
School Type	Secondary; Day
Enrolment	151 boys; 149 girls
Denomination	Roman Catholic
Fees	No

Scariff Community College

Address	Scariff, Co. Clare
Telephone	061-921083
Email	scariffcommunitycollege@eircom.net
Principal	P. J. Mason
School Type	Vocational; Day
Enrolment	131 boys; 153 girls
Denomination	Interdenominational
Fees	No

Shannon Comprehensive School

Address	Shannon, Co. Clare
Telephone	061-361428
Email	admin@scnp.ie
Principal	Margaret O'Connell
School Type	Comprehensive; Day
Enrolment	238 boys; 264 girls
Denomination	Interdenominational
Fees	No

St Joseph's Secondary School

Address	Tulla, Co. Clare
Telephone	065-6835113
Email	admin@sjt.ie
Principal	James Cooney
School Type	Secondary; Day
Enrolment	208 boys; 221 girls
Denomination	Roman Catholic
Fees	No

St Caimin's Community School

Address	Tullyvarraga, Shannon, Co. Clare
Telephone	061-364211
Email	info@stcaimins.ie
Principal	Mary Hanley
School Type	Community; Day
Enrolment	334 boys; 347 girls
Denomination	Interdenominational
Fees	No

Coláiste Daibheid

Address	An t-Ardan Theas, Corcaigh
Telephone	021-4319016
Email	colaistedaibheid@eircom.net
Principal	Diarmuid P Ó Luasa
School Type	Vocational; Day; All tuition through Irish
Enrolment	39 boys; 98 girls
Denomination	Interdenominational
Fees	No

Gaelcholáiste Mhuire

Address	An Mhainistir Thuaidh, Corcaigh
Telephone	021-4307579
Email	scoilmhuireag.ias@tinet.ie
Principal	Dónal Ó Gráda
School Type	Secondary; Day; All tuition through Irish
Enrolment	216 boys; 35 girls
Denomination	Roman Catholic
Fees	No

Ashton School

Address	Blackrock Road, Cork
Telephone	021-4966044
Email	ashton@iol.ie
Principal	C R Payne
School Type	Community; Day
Enrolment	279 boys; 239 girls
Denomination	Church of Ireland
Fees	No

CORK

Bishopstown Community School

Address	Bishopstown, Cork
Telephone	021-4544311
Email	btowncom@iol.ie
Principal	Pat McDonnell
School Type	Community; Day
Enrolment	144 boys; 85 girls
Denomination	Interdenominational
Fees	No

Christ King Girls' Secondary School

Address	South Douglas Road, Cork
Telephone	021-4961448
Email	admin@christkingschool.com
Principal	Kathleen Feeney
School Type	Secondary; Day
Enrolment	1,001 girls
Denomination	Roman Catholic
Fees	No

Christian Brothers College

Address	Sidney Hill, Wellington Road, Cork
Telephone	021-4501653
Email	christianscork@eircom.net
Principal	Dr Laurence A. Jordan
School Type	Secondary; Day
Enrolment	840 boys
Denomination	Roman Catholic
Fees	Yes

Coláiste An Spioraid Naoimh

Address	Bishopstown, Cork
Telephone	021-4543790
Email	info@csncork.ie
Principal	Frank McCarthy
School Type	Secondary; Day
Enrolment	652 boys
Denomination	Roman Catholic
Fees	No

Coláiste Chríost Rí

Address	Capwell Road, Cork
Telephone	021-4274904
Email	info@colaistechriostri.com
Principal	Tomás Ó Caoimh
School Type	Secondary; Day; At least one subject other than Irish taught through Irish
Enrolment	707 boys
Denomination	Roman Catholic
Fees	No

Coláiste Stiofán Naofa

Address	Tramore Road, Cork
Telephone	021-4961020
Email	info@csn.ie
Principal	Tim Kelleher
School Type	Vocational; Day
Enrolment	428 boys; 478 girls
Denomination	Interdenominational
Fees	No

Deerpark CBS

Address	St. Patrick's Close, Cork
Telephone	021-4962025
Email	deerparkcbs@eircom.net
Principal	Mike Ó Floinn
School Type	Secondary; Day
Enrolment	245 boys
Denomination	Roman Catholic
Fees	No

Douglas Community School

Address	Clermont Avenue, Douglas, Cork
Telephone	021-4294201
Email	admin@dcscork.ie
Principal	Bernard E Horgan
School Type	Community; Day
Enrolment	611 boys
Denomination	Interdenominational
Fees	No

Mayfield Community School

Address	Old Youghal Road, Mayfield, Cork
Telephone	021-4506855
Email	admin@mayfieldcommunityschool.ie
Principal	Tony Walsh
School Type	Community; Day
Enrolment	275 boys; 166 girls
Denomination	Interdenominational
Fees	No

Mount Mercy College

Address	Model Farm Road, Cork
Telephone	021-4542366
Email	admin@mountmercy.ie
Principal	Padraigín Uí Riordain
School Type	Secondary; Day
Enrolment	666 girls
Denomination	Roman Catholic
Fees	No

Nagle Community College

Address	Mahon, Blackrock, Cork
Telephone	021-4358633
Email	naglecc@eircom.net
Principal	Anthony Canniffe
School Type	Vocational; Day
Enrolment	225 boys
Denomination	Interdenominational
Fees	No

North Monastery Secondary School

Address	Our Lady's Mount, North Monastery Road, Cork
Telephone	021-4301318
Email	northmonastery.ias@eircom.net
Principal	Anthony O'Loughlin
School Type	Secondary; Day
Enrolment	446 boys
Denomination	Roman Catholic
Fees	No

North Presentation

Address	Farranree, Cork
Telephone	021-4303330
Email	northpres@eircom.net
Principal	Ciaran Cooke
School Type	Secondary; Day
Enrolment	341 girls
Denomination	Roman Catholic
Fees	No

Presentation College

Address	Mardyke, Cork
Telephone	021-4272743
Email	info@pbc-cork.ie
Principal	Michael Hennessy
School Type	Secondary; Day
Enrolment	671 boys
Denomination	Roman Catholic
Fees	Yes

Presentation Secondary School

Address	Joe Murphy Road, Ballyphehane, Cork
Telephone	021-496765
Email	pssgrick@iol.ie
Principal	Sr Sheila Kelleher
School Type	Secondary; Day
Enrolment	426 girls
Denomination	Roman Catholic
Fees	No

Regina Mundi College

Address	Douglas Road, Cork
Telephone	021-4291681
Email	regmun@indigo.ie
Principal	Michael O'Mahony
School Type	Secondary; Day
Enrolment	253 girls
Denomination	Roman Catholic
Fees	No

Scoil Mhuire

Address	2 Sydney Place, Wellington Road, Cork
Telephone	021-4501844
Email	scoilmhuirecork@eircom.net
Principal	Regina Moran
School Type	Secondary; Day
Enrolment	421 girls
Denomination	Roman Catholic
Fees	Yes

St Aloysius School

Address	St Maries Of The Isle, South Crawford Street, Cork
Telephone	021-4316017
Email	stals.ias@eircom.net
Principal	Vivien Fitzgerald-Smith
School Type	Secondary; Day
Enrolment	347 girls
Denomination	Roman Catholic
Fees	No

St Angela's College

Address	St Patrick's Hill, Cork
Telephone	021-4500059
Email	sac@iol.ie
Principal	Rosalie Moloney
School Type	Secondary; Day
Enrolment	520 girls
Denomination	Roman Catholic
Fees	No

St Patrick's College

Address	Gardiner's Hill, Blackrock, Cork
Telephone	021-4503055
Email	stpatrickscollege@hotmail.com
Principal	John Ring
School Type	Secondary; Day
Enrolment	173 girls
Denomination	Roman Catholic
Fees	No

St Vincent's Secondary School

Address	St Mary's Road, Cork
Telephone	021-4307730
Email	vincentprincipal@eircom.net
Principal	Donnchadh Ó Bríain
School Type	Secondary; Day
Enrolment	520 girls
Denomination	Roman Catholic
Fees	No

Terence MacSwiney Community College

Address	Hollyhill, Knocknaheeny, Cork
Telephone	021-4397740
Email	terencemacswineycc@eircom.net
Principal	A. O'Neill
School Type	Vocational; Day
Enrolment	161 boys; 207 girls
Denomination	Interdenominational
Fees	No

Ursuline Secondary School

Address	Blackrock, Cork
Telephone	021-4358012
Email	administration@urscorkb.ie
Principal	Sr Mary McDaid
School Type	Secondary; Day
Enrolment	329 girls
Denomination	Roman Catholic
Fees	No

Coláiste Ghobnatan

Address	Baile Mhic Ire, Co. Chorcaí
Telephone	026-45058
Email	oifig@colaisteghobnatan.ie
Principal	Breandán Ó Lionáird
School Type	Vocational; Day; All tuition through Irish
Enrolment	93 boys; 103 girls
Denomination	Interdenominational
Fees	No

CO. CORK

Ballincollig Community School

Address	Innishmore, Ballincollig, Co. Cork
Telephone	021-4871740
Email	info@balcs.ie
Principal	Kathleen Lowney
School Type	Community; Day
Enrolment	294 boys; 294 girls
Denomination	Interdenominational
Fees	No

Coláiste Choilm

Address	Ballincollig, Co. Cork
Telephone	021-4873308
Email	choilm@eircom.net
Principal	Pat Kinsella
School Type	Vocational; Day; One stream has all tuition through Irish
Enrolment	599 boys; 600 girls
Denomination	Interdenominational
Fees	No

Hamilton High School

Address	Allen Square, Bandon, Co. Cork
Telephone	023-44227
Email	hhs@eircom.net
Principal	James Costelloe
School Type	Secondary; Day
Enrolment	212 boys
Denomination	Roman Catholic
Fees	No

Bandon Grammar School

Address	Bandon, Co. Cork
Telephone	023-41713
Email	info@bandongrammar.ie
Principal	Ian F. Coombes
School Type	Secondary; Day & Boarding
Enrolment	248 boys; 202 girls
Denomination	Church of Ireland
Fees	Day Yes Boarding Yes

Coláiste na Toirbhirte

Address	Ard Aoibhinn, Bandon, Co. Cork
Telephone	023-41814
Email	colnato@eircom.net
Principal	Frances O'Mahony
School Type	Secondary; Day
Enrolment	609 girls
Denomination	Roman Catholic
Fees	No

St Brogan's College

Address	Kilbrogan, Bandon, Co. Cork
Telephone	023-41120
Email	brogansvec@eircom.net
Principal	Eileen C. Corkery
School Type	Vocational; Day
Enrolment	472 boys; 164 girls
Denomination	Interdenominational
Fees	No

Ardscoil Phobal Bheanntrai

Address	Bantry, Co. Cork
Telephone	027-50424
Email	aspb@eircom.net
Principal	Sean Kelly
School Type	Secondary; Day
Enrolment	70 boys; 122 girls
Denomination	Roman Catholic
Fees	No

St Goban's College

Address	Sheskin, Bantry, Co. Cork
Telephone	027-50882
Email	mainstg@eircom.net
Principal	Noreen Deasy
School Type	Vocational; Day
Enrolment	217 boys; 188 girls
Denomination	Interdenominational
Fees	No

Scoil Mhuire

Address	Béal Atha an Ghaorthaidh, Co. Chorcaí
Telephone	026-47050
Email	donncha.ias@eircom.net
Principal	Caoimhín Ó Buachalla
School Type	Vocational; Day; All tuition through Irish
Enrolment	41 boys; 41 girls
Denomination	Interdenominational
Fees	No

Scoil Mhuire Gan Smal

Address	Blarney, Co. Cork
Telephone	021-4385331
Email	blarney@iol.ie
Principal	Joe Whyte
School Type	Secondary; Day
Enrolment	207 boys; 250 girls
Denomination	Roman Catholic
Fees	No

Boherbue Comprehensive School

Address	Boherbue, Mallow, Co. Cork
Telephone	029-76032
Email	boherbue1.ias@eircom.net
Principal	Sean Ó Celleachair
School Type	Comprehensive; Day
Enrolment	214 boys; 200 girls
Denomination	Interdenominational
Fees	No

Coláiste an Chroí Naofa

Address	Carraig na bhFear, Co. Chorcaí
Telephone	021-4884104
Email	sacredhc.ias@eircom.net
Principal	Eamonn Ó Donnabháin
School Type	Secondary; Day
Enrolment	232 boys; 162 girls
Denomination	Roman Catholic
Fees	No

Carrigaline Community School

Address	Waterpark Road, Carrigaline, Co. Cork
Telephone	021-4372300
Email	info@carrigcs.ie
Principal	Donal Murray
School Type	Community; Day
Enrolment	440 boys; 472 girls
Denomination	Interdenominational
Fees	No

St Aloysius College

Address	Carrigtwohill, Co. Cork
Telephone	021-4883341
Email	staloysiuscollege@eircom.net
Principal	Tony Lee
School Type	Secondary; Day
Enrolment	659 girls
Denomination	Roman Catholic
Fees	No

Beara Community School

Address	Castletownbere, Co. Cork
Telephone	027-70177
Email	beara2@eircom.net
Principal	Mary O'Sullivan
School Type	Community; Day
Enrolment	171 boys; 166 girls
Denomination	Interdenominational
Fees	No

Mannix College

Address	Charleville, Co. Cork
Telephone	063-81422
Email	mannixcollege@tinet.ie
Principal	Kevin Whyte
School Type	Vocational; Day
Enrolment	109 boys; 57 girls
Denomination	Interdenominational
Fees	No

Scoil na mBráithre Chríostaí

Address	Bakers Road, Charleville, Co. Cork
Telephone	063-81789
Email	cbscharleville@eircom.net
Principal	Thomas Clarke
School Type	Secondary; Day
Enrolment	213 boys
Denomination	Roman Catholic
Fees	No

St Mary's Secondary School

Address	Convent of Mercy, Charleville, Co. Cork
Telephone	063-81877
Email	stmaryscharleville@eircom.net
Principal	Ann Doherty
School Type	Secondary; Day
Enrolment	381 girls
Denomination	Roman Catholic
Fees	No

Coláiste Mhuire

Address	Cill na Mullach, Co. Chorcaí
Telephone	022-23733
Email	cpnm@eircom.net
Principal	Carol O'Mahony
School Type	Vocational; Day
Enrolment	84 boys; 82 girls
Denomination	Interdenominational
Fees	No

Clonakilty Community College

Address	Clonakilty, Co. Cork
Telephone	023-33877
Email	clonccof@eircom.net
Principal	John P. Duggan
School Type	Vocational; Day
Enrolment	462 boys; 112 girls
Denomination	Interdenominational
Fees	No

Sacred Heart Secondary School

Address	Convent of Mercy, Clonakilty, Co. Cork
Telephone	023-33737
Email	sacredheart@eircom.net
Principal	Sr Eilis McGrath
School Type	Secondary; Day & Boarding
Enrolment	438 girls
Denomination	Roman Catholic
Fees	Day No Boarding Yes

Coachford College

Address	Coachford, Co. Cork
Telephone	021-7334113
Email	coachfordcollege@eircom.net
Principal	Patrick O'Connor
School Type	Vocational; Day
Enrolment	323 boys; 277 girls
Denomination	Interdenominational
Fees	No

Cobh Community College

Address	Carrignafoy, Cobh, Co. Cork
Telephone	021-4811325
Email	cobhcc@eircom.net
Principal	John Russell
School Type	Vocational; Day; At least one subject other than Irish taught through Irish
Enrolment	131 boys; 171 girls
Denomination	Interdenominational
Fees	No

Coláiste Mhuire

Address	Bishop's Street, Cobh, Co. Cork
Telephone	021-4813800
Email	cmuirecobh@eircom.net
Principal	Paula Sweeney
School Type	Secondary; Day
Enrolment	292 boys; 254 girls
Denomination	Roman Catholic
Fees	No

Coláiste Mhuire

Address	Crosshaven, Co. Cork
Telephone	021-4831604
Email	cmuire.ias@eircom.net
Principal	Donal O'Brien
School Type	Secondary; Day
Enrolment	167 boys; 203 girls
Denomination	Roman Catholic
Fees	No

Nagle Rice Secondary School

Address	Doneraile, Co. Cork
Telephone	022-24500
Email	horseclose.ias@eircom.net
Principal	William P. Hallihan
School Type	Secondary; Day
Enrolment	206 boys; 177 girls
Denomination	Roman Catholic
Fees	No

St Aidan's Community College

Address	Ballincolly, Dublin Hill, Cork
Telephone	021-4309598
Email	aidanscork@eircom.net
Principal	Liam Ahern
School Type	Vocational; Day
Enrolment	260 boys; 192 girls
Denomination	Interdenominational
Fees	No

Maria Immaculata Community College

Address	Dunmanway, Co. Cork
Telephone	023-56030
Email	info@micc.ie
Principal	Pat McKelvey
School Type	Vocational; Day
Enrolment	305 boys; 325 girls
Denomination	Interdenominational
Fees	No

Coláiste an Chraoibhin

Address	Duntaheen Road, Fermoy, Co. Cork
Telephone	025-31633
Email	jhennessy@c-chraoibhin.ie
Principal	John Hennessy
School Type	Vocational; Day; One stream has all tuition through Irish
Enrolment	310 boys; 268 girls
Denomination	Interdenominational
Fees	No

Loreto Secondary School

Address	Fermoy, Co. Cork
Telephone	025-32124
Email	principalloretofermoy@eircom.net
Principal	Mary Ryan
School Type	Secondary; Day
Enrolment	625 girls
Denomination	Roman Catholic
Fees	No

Glanmire Community College

Address	Riverstown, Glanmire, Co. Cork
Telephone	021-4822377
Email	gmirecol@eircom.net
Principal	John Fitzgibbons
School Type	Vocational; Day
Enrolment	442 boys; 306 girls
Denomination	Interdenominational
Fees	No

Coláiste An Phiarsaigh

Address	Gleann Maghair, Co. Chorcaí	
Telephone	021-4821955	
Email	colanphiarsaigh@eircom.net	
Principal	Eóin Ó Tuama	
School Type	Secondary; Day & Boarding; All tuition through Irish	
Enrolment	201 boys; 274 girls	
Denomination	Roman Catholic	
Fees	Day No	Boarding Yes

Coláiste Treasa

Address	Kanturk, Co. Cork
Telephone	029-50062
Email	ctkanturk@eircom.net
Principal	Frank O'Sullivan
School Type	Vocational; Day
Enrolment	237 boys; 219 girls
Denomination	Interdenominational
Fees	No

Scoil Mhuire

Address	Kanturk, Co. Cork
Telephone	029-50807
Email	mercyed@eircom.net
Principal	Ted O'Connor
School Type	Secondary; Day
Enrolment	118 boys; 149 girls
Denomination	Roman Catholic
Fees	No

Kinsale Community School

Address	Kinsale, Co. Cork
Telephone	021-4773174
Email	info@kinsalecommunityschool.ie
Principal	Sr Mary Donovan
School Type	Community; Day
Enrolment	264 boys; 294 girls
Denomination	Interdenominational
Fees	No

De La Salle College

Address	Macroom, Co. Cork
Telephone	026-41832
Email	prdlsmac@tinet.ie
Principal	Noel Dunne
School Type	Secondary; Day
Enrolment	283 boys
Denomination	Roman Catholic
Fees	No

McEgan College

Address	Macroom, Co. Cork
Telephone	026-41076
Email	mcegan@iol.ie
Principal	Helen Cadogan
School Type	Vocational; Day
Enrolment	96 boys; 102 girls
Denomination	Interdenominational
Fees	No

St Mary's Secondary School

Address	Convent of Mercy, Macroom, Co. Cork
Telephone	026-41544
Email	adminstmarys@eircom.net
Principal	Anne McGrath
School Type	Secondary; Day
Enrolment	327 girls
Denomination	Roman Catholic
Fees	No

Coláiste Cholmáin

Address	Mainistir Fhearmuí, Co. Chorcaí
Telephone	025-31930
Email	info@stcolmansfermoy.com
Principal	John Hickson
School Type	Secondary; Day
Enrolment	357 boys
Denomination	Roman Catholic
Fees	No

Patrician Academy

Address	Mallow, Co. Cork
Telephone	022-21884
Email	admin@patricianacademy.com
Principal	Ann Dunne
School Type	Secondary; Day
Enrolment	356 boys
Denomination	Roman Catholic
Fees	No

St Mary's Secondary School

Address	Convent of Mercy, Mallow, Co. Cork
Telephone	022-21998
Email	stmarysmallow@eircom.net
Principal	Sr Brigid Biggane
School Type	Secondary; Day
Enrolment	539 girls
Denomination	Roman Catholic
Fees	No

Christian Brothers Secondary School

Address	Castleredmond, Midleton, Co. Cork
Telephone	021-4631555
Email	cbssecmidleton@eircom.net
Principal	Denis J. Ring
School Type	Secondary; Day
Enrolment	398 boys
Denomination	Roman Catholic
Fees	No

Midleton College

Address	Midleton, Co. Cork
Telephone	021-4631146
Email	info@midletoncollege.ie
Principal	Simon Thompson
School Type	Secondary; Day & Boarding
Enrolment	158 boys; 121 girls
Denomination	Church of Ireland
Fees	Day Yes Boarding Yes

St Colman's Community College

Address	Youghal Road, Midleton, Co. Cork
Telephone	021-4631696
Email	stcolman@midletonvec.ie
Principal	Tom Hughes
School Type	Vocational; Day
Enrolment	365 boys; 234 girls
Denomination	Interdenominational
Fees	No

St Mary's High School

Address	Midleton, Co. Cork
Telephone	021-4631973
Email	stmarysm@iol.ie
Principal	Donal Cronin
School Type	Secondary; Day
Enrolment	530 girls
Denomination	Roman Catholic
Fees	No

Millstreet Community School

Address	Millstreet Town, Co. Cork
Telephone	029-70087
Email	mcsmar@eircom.net
Principal	Patrick Pigott
School Type	Community; Day
Enrolment	144 boys; 170 girls
Denomination	Interdenominational
Fees	No

Christian Brothers Secondary School

Address	Mitchelstown, Co. Cork
Telephone	025-24104
Email	donnchac@eircom.net
Principal	Donncha Crowley
School Type	Secondary; Day
Enrolment	274 boys
Denomination	Roman Catholic
Fees	No

Presentation Secondary School

Address	Mitchelstown, Co. Cork
Telephone	025-24394
Email	annekirke.ias@eircom.net
Principal	Anne Kirke
School Type	Secondary; Day
Enrolment	275 girls
Denomination	Roman Catholic
Fees	No

St Fanahan's College

Address	Mitchelstown, Co. Cork
Telephone	025-24314
Email	gercanning2004@eircom.net
Principal	Geraldine Canning
School Type	Vocational; Day
Enrolment	113 boys; 121 girls
Denomination	Interdenominational
Fees	No

St Peter's Community School

Address	Passage West, Co. Cork
Telephone	021-4841599
Email	stpeter@iol.ie
Principal	D. Aherne
School Type	Community; Day
Enrolment	167 boys; 225 girls
Denomination	Interdenominational
Fees	No

St Francis Capuchin College

Address	Rochestown, Co. Cork
Telephone	021-4891417
Email	rococoll.ias@eircom.net
Principal	Diarmuid Ó Mathuna
School Type	Secondary; Day
Enrolment	196 boys
Denomination	Roman Catholic
Fees	No

Mount St Michael

Address	Rosscarbery, Co. Cork
Telephone	023-48114
Email	rossnet@iol.ie
Principal	Bart Kerrisk
School Type	Secondary; Day & Boarding
Enrolment	228 boys; 209 girls
Denomination	Roman Catholic
Fees	Day No Boarding Yes

Schull Community College

Address	Colla Road, Schull, Co. Cork
Telephone	028-28315
Email	office@schullcommunitycollege.com
Principal	Timothy O'Connor
School Type	Vocational; Day
Enrolment	222 boys; 225 girls
Denomination	Interdenominational
Fees	No

Mercy Heights Secondary School

Address	Skibbereen, Co. Cork
Telephone	028-21550
Email	mercyhts@iol.ie
Principal	Anton O'Mahony
School Type	Secondary; Day
Enrolment	427 girls
Denomination	Roman Catholic
Fees	No

Rossa College

Address	Skibbereen, Co. Cork
Telephone	028-21644
Email	rossacollege@eircom.net
Principal	John O'Brien
School Type	Vocational Day
Enrolment	86 boys; 111 girls
Denomination	Interdenominational
Fees	No

St Fachtna's – De La Salle College

Address	Skibbereen, Co. Cork
Telephone	028-21454
Email	sfdls@eircom.net
Principal	Cathal O'Donovan
School Type	Secondary; Day
Enrolment	305 boys
Denomination	Roman Catholic
Fees	No

Davis College

Address	Annabelle, Summerhill, Co. Cork
Telephone	022-21173
Email	davisoff@tinet.ie
Principal	Denis Healy
School Type	Vocational; Day; At least one subject other than Irish taught through Irish
Enrolment	232 boys; 333 girls
Denomination	Interdenominational
Fees	No

Christian Brothers School

Address	Golf Links Road, Youghal, Co. Cork
Telephone	024-92185
Email	kgroeger@iol.ie
Principal	Kieran Groeger
School Type	Secondary; Day
Enrolment	229 boys
Denomination	Roman Catholic
Fees	No

Coláiste Eoin

Address	Golf Links Road, Youghal, Co. Cork
Telephone	024-92804
Email	colaisteeoin@eircom.net
Principal	Sean Ó Brosnacháin
School Type	Vocational; Day; At least one subject other than Irish taught through Irish
Enrolment	199 boys; 181 girls
Denomination	Interdenominational
Fees	No

Loreto Secondary School

Address	Youghal, Co. Cork
Telephone	024-92709
Email	marycrotty@eircom.net
Principal	Mary Crotty
School Type	Secondary; Day
Enrolment	288 girls
Denomination	Roman Catholic
Fees	No

Gairmscoil Mhic Diarmada

Address	An Leadhbgarbh, Arainn Mhór, Co. Donegal
Telephone	074-9520747
Email	gsmhicd@donegalvec.ie
Principal	Poilín Ní Chormaic
School Type	Vocational; Day
Enrolment	25 boys; 19 girls
Denomination	Interdenominational
Fees	No

Coláiste Cholmcille

Address	College Street, Ballyshannon, Co. Donegal
Telephone	071-9858288
Email	jimmykeogh@eircom.net
Principal	Jimmy Keogh
School Type	Community; Day
Enrolment	329 boys; 346 girls
Denomination	Interdenominational
Fees	No

Crana College

Address	Crana Road, Buncrana, Co. Donegal
Telephone	074-9361113
Email	cranacollege@donegalvec.ie
Principal	Mary McLaughlin
School Type	Vocational; Day
Enrolment	124 boys; 132 girls
Denomination	Interdenominational
Fees	No

CO. DONEGAL

Scoil Mhuire

Address	St. Oran's Road, Buncrana, Co. Donegal
Telephone	074-9361065
Email	mercybuncrana.ias@tinet.ie
Principal	Liam Rainey
School Type	Secondary; Day
Enrolment	346 boys; 376 girls
Denomination	Roman Catholic
Fees	No

Magh Ene College

Address	Bundoran, Co. Donegal
Telephone	071-9841364
Email	mecvec@eircom.net
Principal	John McLean
School Type	Vocational; Day
Enrolment	166 boys; 164 girls
Denomination	Interdenominational
Fees	No

Carrick Vocational School

Address	Carrick, Co. Donegal
Telephone	073-39071
Email	carrickvs@donegalvec.ie
Principal	Tony Bonar
School Type	Vocational; Day
Enrolment	115 boys; 97 girls
Denomination	Interdenominational
Fees	No

Abbey Vocational School

Address	Donegal Town, Co. Donegal
Telephone	074-9721105
Email	abbeyvc@donegalvec.ie
Principal	Mary Ann Kane
School Type	Vocational; Day
Enrolment	399 boys; 452 girls
Denomination	Interdenominational
Fees	No

Rosses Community School

Address	Dungloe, Co. Donegal
Telephone	074-9521122
Email	danielgallagherrcs@eircom.net
Principal	Daniel J. Gallagher
School Type	Community; Day
Enrolment	181 boys; 173 girls
Denomination	Interdenominational
Fees	No

St Columba's Comprehensive School

Address	Glenties, Co. Donegal
Telephone	074-9551172
Email	glenties@indigo.ie
Principal	Michael Naughton
School Type	Comprehensive; Day
Enrolment	238 boys; 235 girls
Denomination	Interdenominational
Fees	No

St Catherine's Vocational School

Address	Donegal Road, Killybegs, Co. Donegal
Telephone	074-9731491
Email	stcath@iol.ie
Principal	Joseph Ward
School Type	Vocational; Day
Enrolment	158 boys; 190 girls
Denomination	Interdenominational
Fees	No

Coláiste Ailigh

Address	Bóthar Ard, Leitir Ceanainn, Co. Donegal
Telephone	074-9125943
Email	colaisteailigh@donegalvec.ie
Principal	Michéal Ó Giobúin
School Type	Vocational; Day; All tuition through Irish
Enrolment	42 boys; 87 girls
Denomination	Interdenominational
Fees	No

Pobalscoil Chloich Cheannfhaola

Address	An Fálcarrach, Leitir Ceanainn, Co. Dhún na nGall
Telephone	074-9135424
Email	pccfalc@eircom.net
Principal	Pádraig Mac A Bhíocaire
School Type	Community; Day
Enrolment	346 boys; 295 girls
Denomination	Interdenominational
Fees	No

Pobalscoil Ghaoth Dobhair

Address	Doirí Beaga, Leitir Ceannain, Tír Chonaill
Telephone	074-9531311
Email	pobalscoilgd.ias@eircom.net
Principal	Noel Ó Gallchoir
School Type	Community; Day; All tuition through Irish
Enrolment	164 boys; 168 girls
Denomination	Interdenominational
Fees	No

Letterkenny Vocational School

Address	Windyhall, Letterkenny, Co. Donegal
Telephone	074-9121047
Email	letterkennyvs@donegalvec.ie
Principal	Patrick O'Connor
School Type	Vocational; Day
Enrolment	161 boys; 188 girls
Denomination	Interdenominational
Fees	No

Loreto Convent

Address	Letterkenny, Co. Donegal
Telephone	074-9121850
Email	lorcondl@iol.ie
Principal	Sr Siobhan Ní Chuill
School Type	Secondary; Day
Enrolment	944 girls
Denomination	Roman Catholic
Fees	No

Mulroy College

Address	Milford, Letterkenny, Co. Donegal
Telephone	074-9153346
Email	mulroycollege@donegalvec.ie
Principal	Rita Gleeson
School Type	Vocational; Day
Enrolment	288 boys; 167 girls
Denomination	Interdenominational
Fees	No

St Eunan's College

Address	Letterkenny, Co. Donegal
Telephone	074-9121143
Email	steunansadmin@eircom.net
Principal	Rev. Michael Carney
School Type	Secondary; Day
Enrolment	810 boys
Denomination	Roman Catholic
Fees	No

Carndonagh Community School

Address	Carndonagh, Lifford, Co. Donegal
Telephone	074-9374260
Email	ccsoffice@eircom.net
Principal	Paul Fiorentini
School Type	Community; Day
Enrolment	495 boys; 578 girls
Denomination	Interdenominational
Fees	No

Deele College

Address	Raphoe, Lifford, Co. Donegal
Telephone	074-9145493
Email	deelecoll@eircom.net
Principal	P. J. McGowan
School Type	Vocational; Day
Enrolment	203 boys; 233 girls
Denomination	Interdenominational
Fees	No

Gairmscoil Chú Uladh

Address	Béal an Átha Móir, An Clochán, Leifear, Co. Donegal
Telephone	074-9546133
Email	gcu@donegalvec.ie
Principal	Fiona Ni Chnáimhsí
School Type	Vocational; Day; All tuition through Irish
Enrolment	56 boys; 60 girls
Denomination	Interdenominational
Fees	No

St Columba's College

Address	Stranorlar, Lifford, Co. Donegal
Telephone	074-9131246
Email	stcolumbascollege1@eircom.net
Principal	Gerry Bennett
School Type	Secondary; Day
Enrolment	352 boys; 412 girls
Denomination	Roman Catholic
Fees	No

Vocational School

Address	Main Street, Stranorlar, Lifford, Co. Donegal
Telephone	074-9131083
Email	svs@eircom.net
Principal	Frank Dooley
School Type	Vocational; Day
Enrolment	194 boys; 125 girls
Denomination	Interdenominational
Fees	No

Loreto Community School

Address	Milford, Co. Donegal
Telephone	074-9153399
Email	admin@loretomilford.com
Principal	Andrew Kelly
School Type	Community; Day
Enrolment	196 boys; 282 girls
Denomination	Interdenominational
Fees	No

Moville Community College

Address	Carrownaff, Moville, Co. Donegal
Telephone	074-9385988
Email	moville@donegalvec.ie
Principal	Anthony Doogan
School Type	Vocational; Day
Enrolment	204 boys; 186 girls
Denomination	Interdenominational
Fees	No

Coláiste Phobail Cholmcille

Address	Baile Ur, Oilean Thorai, Co. Dhun na nGall
Telephone	074-9165448
Email	-------
Principal	Máire Clár Nic Mhathúna
School Type	Vocational; Day; All tuition through Irish
Enrolment	9 boys; 11 girls
Denomination	Interdenominational
Fees	No

The Royal and Prior School

Address	Raphoe, Co. Donegal
Telephone	074-9145389
Email	admin@royalandprior.ie
Principal	D. G. West
School Type	Secondary; Day and Boarding
Enrolment	281 boys; 333 girls
Denomination	Church of Ireland
Fees	Day No Boarding Yes

Belvedere College

Address	6 Great Denmark Street, Dublin 1
Telephone	01-8586600
Email	admin@sj.belvederecollege.ie
Principal	Gerard Foley
School Type	Secondary; Day
Enrolment	867 boys
Denomination	Roman Catholic
Fees	Yes

DUBLIN

Larkin Community College

Address	Cathal Brugha Street, Dublin 1
Telephone	01-8741913
Email	janet.rooney@lcc.cdvec.ie
Principal	Noel O'Brien
School Type	Vocational; Day
Enrolment	186 boys; 151 girls
Denomination	Interdenominational
Fees	No

Mount Carmel Secondary School

Address	Kings Inn Street, Dublin 1
Telephone	01-8730958
Email	mtcarmel@eircom.net
Principal	Sr Teresa McAllister
School Type	Secondary; Day
Enrolment	277 girls
Denomination	Roman Catholic
Fees	No

O'Connell School

Address	North Richmond Street, Dublin 1
Telephone	01-8748307
Email	secretary@oconnell.iol.ie
Principal	Michael Finucane
School Type	Secondary; Day
Enrolment	322 boys; 23 girls
Denomination	Roman Catholic
Fees	No

Catholic University School

Address	89 Lower Leeson Street, Dublin 2
Telephone	01-6762586
Email	office@cus.ie
Principal	Fr Martin Daly
School Type	Secondary; Day
Enrolment	430 boys
Denomination	Roman Catholic
Fees	Yes

CBS Westland Row

Address	Westland Row, Dublin 2
Telephone	01-6614143
Email	westlandrowcbs@eircom.net
Principal	Ken Duggan
School Type	Secondary; Day
Enrolment	58 boys; 59 girls
Denomination	Roman Catholic
Fees	No

Loreto College

Address	53 St Stephens Green, Dublin 2
Telephone	01-6618179
Email	thegreen.ias@eircom.net
Principal	Tríona Barrett
School Type	Secondary; Day
Enrolment	551 girls
Denomination	Roman Catholic
Fees	Yes

Holy Faith Secondary School

Address	1 Belgrove Road, Clontarf, Dublin 3
Telephone	01-8331507
Email	hfc.ias@eircom.net
Principal	Deirdre Gogarty
School Type	Secondary; Day
Enrolment	589 girls
Denomination	Roman Catholic
Fees	No

Marino College

Address	14-20 Marino Mart, Fairview, Dublin 3
Telephone	01-8332100
Email	info@marino.cdvec.ie
Principal	James Martin
School Type	Vocational; Day
Enrolment	116 boys; 409 girls
Denomination	Interdenominational
Fees	No

Mount Temple Comprehensive

Address	Malahide Road, Dublin 3
Telephone	01-8336984
Email	temple10@eircom.ie
Principal	Liam Wegimont
School Type	Comprehensive; Day
Enrolment	469 boys; 382 girls
Denomination	Church of Ireland
Fees	No

St Joseph's CBS

Address	Merville Avenue, Fairview, Dublin 3
Telephone	01-8339779
Email	stjoeys.ias@eircom.net
Principal	Brian O'Dwyer
School Type	Secondary; Day
Enrolment	217 boys; 20 girls
Denomination	Roman Catholic
Fees	No

John Scottus Secondary School

Address	74 Morehampton Road, Donnybrook, Dublin 4
Telephone	01-6680828
Email	scottus@gofree.indigo.ie
Principal	Dr Michael Telford
School Type	Secondary; Day
Enrolment	59 boys; 62 girls
Denomination	Interdenominational
Fees	Yes

Marian College

Address	Ballsbridge, Dublin 4
Telephone	01-6684036
Email	pmeany@mariancollege.ie
Principal	Paul Meany
School Type	Secondary; Day
Enrolment	388 boys; 11 girls
Denomination	Roman Catholic
Fees	No

Muckross Park College

Address	Donnybrook, Dublin 4
Telephone	01-2691096
Email	pcfitzsimons@eircom.net
Principal	Patricia Fitzsimons
School Type	Secondary; Day
Enrolment	673 girls
Denomination	Roman Catholic
Fees	No

St Conleth's College

Address	28 Clyde Road, Ballsbridge, Dublin 4
Telephone	01-6680022
Email	sconleth@iol.ie
Principal	Peter Gallagher
School Type	Secondary; Day
Enrolment	211 boys; 20 girls
Denomination	Roman Catholic
Fees	Yes

St Mary's Secondary School

Address	Haddington Road, Dublin 4
Telephone	01-6681951
Email	stmaryshaddingtonroad@eircom.net
Principal	Attracta Quinn
School Type	Secondary; Day
Enrolment	105 girls
Denomination	Roman Catholic
Fees	No

St Michael's College

Address	Ailesbury Road, Dublin 4
Telephone	01-2189400
Email	stmcoll@indigo.ie
Principal	Tim Kelleher
School Type	Secondary; Day
Enrolment	554 boys
Denomination	Roman Catholic
Fees	Yes

Technical Institute

Address	Cambridge Road, Ringsend, Dublin 4
Telephone	01-6684498
Email	info@ringtec.cdvec.ie
Principal	Charles McManus
School Type	Vocational; Day
Enrolment	102 boys; 64 girls
Denomination	Interdenominational
Fees	No

The Teresian School

Address	12 Stillorgan Road, Donnybrook, Dublin 4
Telephone	01-2691376
Email	school@teresian.iol.ie
Principal	Natuca Cordon
School Type	Secondary; Day
Enrolment	180 girls
Denomination	Roman Catholic
Fees	Yes

Ardscoil La Salle

Address	Raheny Road, Raheny, Dublin 5
Telephone	01-8480055
Email	seclasalle@eircom.net
Principal	Stephen Jordan
School Type	Secondary; Day
Enrolment	319 boys; 132 girls
Denomination	Roman Catholic
Fees	No

Chanel College

Address	Coolock, Dublin 5
Telephone	01-8480655
Email	chaneloffice@eircom.net
Principal	Fr John Hand
School Type	Secondary; Day
Enrolment	417 boys
Denomination	Roman Catholic
Fees	No

Greendale Community School

Address	Briarfield Villas, Kilbarrack, Dublin 5
Telephone	01-8322735
Email	admin@greendalecs.com
Principal	Anton Carroll
School Type	Community; Day
Enrolment	98 boys; 95 girls
Denomination	Interdenominational
Fees	No

Manor House

Address	Watermill Road, Raheny, Dublin 5
Telephone	01-8316782
Email	principal@manorhouseschool.com
Principal	Mary O'Neill
School Type	Secondary; Day
Enrolment	803 girls
Denomination	Roman Catholic
Fees	No

Mercy College

Address	St Brendan's Drive, Coolock, Dublin 5
Telephone	01-8480888
Email	info@mercycoolock.ie
Principal	Patricia Dywer
School Type	Secondary; Day
Enrolment	446 girls
Denomination	Roman Catholic
Fees	No

St David's CBS

Address	Malahide Road, Artane, Dublin 5
Telephone	01-8315322
Email	office@stdavidscbs.net
Principal	Padraic Kavanagh
School Type	Secondary; Day
Enrolment	533 boys
Denomination	Roman Catholic
Fees	No

St Mary's Secondary School

Address	Brookwood Meadow, Killester, Dublin 5
Telephone	01-8310963
Email	holyfaith.ias@eircom.net
Principal	Catherine Wyer
School Type	Secondary; Day
Enrolment	522 girls
Denomination	Roman Catholic
Fees	No

St Paul's College

Address	Sybil Hill, Raheny, Dublin 5
Telephone	01-8314011
Email	admin@spaulscollege.ie
Principal	Ciaran McCormack
School Type	Secondary; Day
Enrolment	566 boys
Denomination	Roman Catholic
Fees	No

Alexandra College

Address	Milltown, Dublin 6
Telephone	01-4977571
Email	info@alexandracollege.ie
Principal	Marian Healy
School Type	Secondary; Day & Boarding
Enrolment	618 girls
Denomination	Church of Ireland
Fees	Day Yes Boarding Yes

Gonzaga College

Address	Sandford Road, Ranelagh, Dublin 6
Telephone	01-4972931
Email	headmaster@gonzaga.ie
Principal	Patrick J. W. Potts
School Type	Secondary; Day
Enrolment	516 boys
Denomination	Roman Catholic
Fees	Yes

Sandford Park School

Address	Sandford Road, Ranelagh, Dublin 6
Telephone	01-4971417
Email	admin@sandfordparkschool.ie
Principal	Edith Byrne
School Type	Secondary; Day
Enrolment	244 boys
Denomination	Church of Ireland
Fees	Yes

St Louis High School

Address	Charleville Road, Rathmines, Dublin 6
Telephone	01-4975458
Email	stlouisr@iol.ie
Principal	Mary Morgan
School Type	Secondary; Day
Enrolment	610 girls
Denomination	Roman Catholic
Fees	No

St Mary's College

Address	Rathmines, Dublin 6
Telephone	01-4062100
Email	sensec@stmarys.ie
Principal	Clive Byrne
School Type	Secondary; Day
Enrolment	458 boys
Denomination	Roman Catholic
Fees	Yes

Stratford College

Address	1 Zion Road, Rathgar, Dublin 6
Telephone	01-4922315
Email	admin@stratfordcollege.ie
Principal	Patricia Gordon
School Type	Secondary; Day
Enrolment	85 boys; 72 girls
Denomination	Jewish
Fees	Yes

The High School

Address	Danum, Zion Road, Rathgar, Dublin 6
Telephone	01-4922611
Email	office@highschool.com
Principal	Brian Duffy
School Type	Secondary; Day
Enrolment	457 boys; 325 girls
Denomination	Church of Ireland
Fees	Yes

Our Lady's School

Address	Templeogue Road, Terenure, Dublin 6W
Telephone	01-4903241
Email	ols@iol.ie
Principal	G. Friel
School Type	Secondary; Day
Enrolment	722 girls
Denomination	Roman Catholic
Fees	No

Presentation College

Address	Terenure, Dublin 6W
Telephone	01-4902404
Email	principal@psst.ie
Principal	Austin Kearney
School Type	Secondary; Day
Enrolment	453 girls
Denomination	Roman Catholic
Fees	No

St Mac Dara's Community College

Address	Wellington Lane, Templeogue, Dublin 6W
Telephone	01-4566216
Email	stmacdaras@eircom.net
Principal	Seamus McPhillips
School Type	Vocational; Day
Enrolment	462 boys; 339 girls
Denomination	Interdenominational
Fees	No

Templeogue College

Address	Templeville Road, Dublin 6W
Telephone	01-4905788
Email	info@templeoguecollege.ie
Principal	Kevin O'Brien
School Type	Secondary; Day
Enrolment	613 boys
Denomination	Roman Catholic
Fees	No

Terenure College

Address	Templeogue Road, Terenure, Dublin 6W
Telephone	01-4904621
Email	admin@terenurecollege.ie
Principal	Fr Eanna Ó hObain
School Type	Secondary; Day
Enrolment	756 boys
Denomination	Roman Catholic
Fees	Yes

Coláiste Eanna

Address	Kilkieran Road, Cabra, Dublin 7
Telephone	01-8389577
Email	info@cec.cdvec.ie
Principal	Alfred J Bryan
School Type	Vocational; Day
Enrolment	73 boys; 81 girls
Denomination	Interdenominational
Fees	No

Coláiste Mhuire

Address	Bothar Rath Tó, Baile Atha Cliath 7
Telephone	01-8688996
Email	po@colaistemhuire.ie
Principal	Daithi O Neill
School Type	Secondary; Day; All tuition through Irish
Enrolment	112 boys; 61 girls
Denomination	Roman Catholic
Fees	No

St Declan's College

Address	Nephin Road, Cabra, Dublin 7
Telephone	01-8380357
Email	info@stdeclanscollege.org
Principal	Jack Cleary
School Type	Secondary; Day
Enrolment	655 boys
Denomination	Roman Catholic
Fees	No

St Dominic's College

Address	Cabra, Dublin 7
Telephone	01-8385282
Email	stdominicscollegeadmin@eircom.net
Principal	Mary Keane
School Type	Secondary; Day
Enrolment	847 girls
Denomination	Roman Catholic
Fees	No

St Joseph's Secondary School

Address	Stanhope Street, Dublin 7
Telephone	01-6710419
Email	stanhope.ias@eircom.net
Principal	Tommy Coyle
School Type	Secondary; Day
Enrolment	246 girls
Denomination	Roman Catholic
Fees	No

St Paul's CBS

Address	CBS, North Brunswick Street, Dublin 7
Telephone	01-8720781
Email	michaelblanchfield@eircom.net
Principal	Michael Blanchfield
School Type	Secondary; Day
Enrolment	239 boys
Denomination	Roman Catholic
Fees	No

CBS James Street

Address	James's Street, Dublin 8
Telephone	01-4547756
Email	jambod8@eircom.net
Principal	William O'Brien
School Type	Secondary; Day
Enrolment	257 boys
Denomination	Roman Catholic
Fees	No

Mercy Secondary School

Address	Goldenbridge, Inchicore, Dublin 8
Telephone	01-4531262
Email	mercysecsch.ias@eircom.net
Principal	Eamonn Corrigan
School Type	Secondary; Day
Enrolment	190 girls
Denomination	Roman Catholic
Fees	No

Presentation College

Address	Warrenmount, Dublin 8
Telephone	01-4547520
Email	warrencmr@eircom.net
Principal	Sr Frances Murphy
School Type	Secondary; Day
Enrolment	281 girls
Denomination	Roman Catholic
Fees	No

St Patrick's Cathedral Grammar School

Address	St Patrick's Close, Dublin 8
Telephone	01-4543388
Email	officepatricksgrammar@eircom.net
Principal	Brian Levis
School Type	Secondary; Day
Enrolment	86 boys; 63 girls
Denomination	Church of Ireland
Fees	Yes

Synge Street CBS

Address	Synge Street, Dublin 8
Telephone	01-4783998
Email	syngestreetoffice@eircom.net
Principal	Michael Minnock
School Type	Secondary; Day
Enrolment	307 boys
Denomination	Roman Catholic
Fees	No

Ardscoil Rís

Address	Griffith Avenue, Dublin 9
Telephone	01-8332633
Email	ard9@eircom.net
Principal	Pat J. Reilly
School Type	Secondary; Day
Enrolment	510 boys
Denomination	Roman Catholic
Fees	No

Dominican College

Address	Griffith Avenue, Drumcondra, Dublin 9
Telephone	01-8376080
Email	dominicancollege2004@eircom.net
Principal	Sr Chanel O'Reilly
School Type	Secondary; Day
Enrolment	680 girls
Denomination	Roman Catholic
Fees	No

Margaret Aylward Community College

Address	The Thatch Road, Whitehall, Dublin 9
Telephone	01-8375712
Email	mary.friel@macc.cdvec.ie
Principal	Mary Friel
School Type	Vocational; Day
Enrolment	150 girls
Denomination	Interdenominational
Fees	No

Maryfield College

Address	Glandore Road, Drumcondra, Dublin 9
Telephone	01-8373574
Email	admin@maryfieldcollege.ie
Principal	Gerard Wrigley
School Type	Secondary; Day
Enrolment	634 girls
Denomination	Roman Catholic
Fees	No

Our Lady of Mercy College

Address	Beaumont, Dublin 9
Telephone	01-8371478
Email	mercybeaumont@eircom.net
Principal	Sr Bonaventure Higgins
School Type	Secondary; Day
Enrolment	299 girls
Denomination	Roman Catholic
Fees	No

Plunket College

Address	Swords Road, Whitehall, Dublin 9
Telephone	01-8371689
Email	info@plunket.cdvec.ie
Principal	Kevin O'Meara
School Type	Vocational; Day
Enrolment	240 boys; 146 girls
Denomination	Interdenominational
Fees	No

Rosmini Community School

Address	Grace Park Road, Drumcondra, Dublin 9
Telephone	01-8371694
Email	info@pobalscoilrosmini.ie
Principal	Ivan O'Callaghan
School Type	Community; Day
Enrolment	346 girls; 64 boys
Denomination	Interdenominational
Fees	No

St Aidan's CBS

Address	Collins Avenue Ext, Whitehall, Dublin 9
Telephone	01-8377587
Email	aidancbs.ias@eircom.net
Principal	James Reynolds
School Type	Secondary; Day
Enrolment	596 boys
Denomination	Roman Catholic
Fees	No

Scoil Chaitríona

Address	Bóthar Mobhí, Glasnaion, Ath Cliath 9
Telephone	01-8370762
Email	scoil_chaitriona@ireland.com
Principal	Caitríona Ní Laighin
School Type	Secondary; Day; All tuition through Irish
Enrolment	157 boys; 179 girls
Denomination	Roman Catholic
Fees	No

Trinity Comprehensive School Ballymun

Address	Ballymun Road, Dublin 9
Telephone	01-8423711
Email	sencomp.ias@eircom.net
Principal	Desmond Kelly
School Type	Comprehensive; Day
Enrolment	350 boys; 426 girls
Denomination	Interdenominational
Fees	No

Caritas College

Address	Drumfinn Road, Ballyfermot, Dublin 10
Telephone	01-6265927
Email	caritascollege.ias@eircom.net
Principal	Adrienne Whelan
School Type	Secondary; Day
Enrolment	392 girls
Denomination	Roman Catholic
Fees	No

Kylemore College

Address	Kylemore Road, Ballyfermot, Dublin 10
Telephone	01-6265901
Email	info@kylemore.cdvec.ie
Principal	Declan MacDaid
School Type	Vocational; Day
Enrolment	298 boys; 96 girls
Denomination	Interdenominational
Fees	No

St Dominic's Secondary School

Address	Ballyfermot, Dublin 10
Telephone	01-6266493
Email	firinne@hotmail.com
Principal	Mary Daly
School Type	Secondary; Day
Enrolment	477 girls
Denomination	Roman Catholic
Fees	No

St John's College De La Salle

Address	Le Fanu Road, Ballyfermot, Dublin 10
Telephone	01-6264943
Email	-------
Principal	Pat McMorrow (Acting)
School Type	Secondary; Day
Enrolment	555 boys
Denomination	Roman Catholic
Fees	No

Beneavin De La Salle College

Address	Beneavin Road Finglas, Dublin 11
Telephone	01-8341410
Email	mcevoysok@eircom.net
Principal	Joe Twomey
School Type	Secondary; Day
Enrolment	428 boys
Denomination	Roman Catholic
Fees	No

Coláiste Eoin

Address	Cappagh Road, Finglas West, Dublin 11
Telephone	01-8341426
Email	info@eoin.cdvec.ie
Principal	Bernadette Hand
School Type	Vocational; Day
Enrolment	153 boys; 118 girls
Denomination	Interdenominational
Fees	No

Coláiste Íde

Address	Cardiffsbridge Road, Finglas West, Dublin 11
Telephone	01-8342333
Email	generalenquiries@ide.cdvec.ie
Principal	Malachy Buckeridge
School Type	Vocational; Day
Enrolment	415 boys; 468 girls
Denomination	Interdenominational
Fees	No

Mater Christi

Address	Cappagh, Finglas, Dublin 11
Telephone	01-8343165
Email	materoffice@eircom.net
Principal	Frank Houlihan
School Type	Secondary; Day
Enrolment	216 girls
Denomination	Roman Catholic
Fees	No

Patrician College

Address	Deanstown Avenue, Finglas West, Dublin 11
Telephone	01-8343067
Email	patricianfinglas.ias@eircom.net
Principal	Michael Stacey
School Type	Secondary; Day
Enrolment	233 boys
Denomination	Roman Catholic
Fees	No

St Kevin's College

Address	Ballygall Road East, Finglas, Dublin 11
Telephone	01-8371423
Email	kevinscoll.ias@eircom.net
Principal	Martin Duggan
School Type	Secondary; Day
Enrolment	260 boys
Denomination	Roman Catholic
Fees	No

St Mary's Secondary School

Address	Holy Faith Convent, Glasnevin, Dublin 11
Telephone	01-8374413
Email	stmarysglasnevin@eircom.net
Principal	Margaret Lennon
School Type	Secondary; Day
Enrolment	656 girls
Denomination	Roman Catholic
Fees	No

St Michael's Secondary School

Address	Wellmount Road, Finglas, Dublin 11
Telephone	01-8341767
Email	stmichaelshfss.ias@eircom.net
Principal	John Barry
School Type	Secondary; Day
Enrolment	489 girls
Denomination	Roman Catholic
Fees	No

St Vincent's CBS Glasnevin

Address	Glasnevin, Dublin 11
Telephone	01-8304375
Email	vincents.ias@tinet.ie
Principal	Timothy Hurley
School Type	Secondary; Day
Enrolment	301 boys
Denomination	Roman Catholic
Fees	No

Assumption Secondary School

Address	Walkinstown, Dublin 12
Telephone	01-4507017
Email	office1aw@eircom.net
Principal	John Costello
School Type	Secondary; Day
Enrolment	395 girls
Denomination	Roman Catholic
Fees	No

Greenhills College

Address	Limekiln Avenue, Greenhills, Dublin 12
Telephone	01-4507779
Email	info@greenhillscollege.ie
Principal	Michael Flatley
School Type	Vocational; Day
Enrolment	331 boys; 119 girls
Denomination	Interdenominational
Fees	No

Loreto College

Address	Crumlin Road, Dublin 12
Telephone	01-4542380
Email	info@loretocrumlin.ie
Principal	Margaret Donagh
School Type	Secondary; Day
Enrolment	528 girls
Denomination	Roman Catholic
Fees	No

Meanscoil Chroimghlinne

Address	314-318 Crumlin Road, Dublin 12
Telephone	01-4556255
Email	eommc.ias@eircom.net
Principal	Etáin Ó Moore
School Type	Secondary; Day
Enrolment	59 boys; 39 girls
Denomination	Roman Catholic
Fees	No

Meanscoil Iognáid Rís

Address	Long Mile Road, Walkinstown, Dublin 12
Telephone	01-4518316
Email	dcbs@eircom.net
Principal	Dr Raymond Walsh
School Type	Secondary; Day
Enrolment	623 boys
Denomination	Roman Catholic
Fees	No

Meanscoil Naomh Colm

Address	Captain's Road, Crumlin, Dublin 12
Telephone	01-4555606
Email	jacinthacbscrumlin@eircom.net
Principal	Mary Dowling-Maher
School Type	Secondary; Day
Enrolment	92 boys
Denomination	Roman Catholic
Fees	No

Our Lady of Mercy Secondary School

Address	Mourne Road, Drimnagh, Dublin 12
Telephone	01-4554691
Email	olm.ias@eircom.net
Principal	Patrick Collings
School Type	Secondary; Day
Enrolment	156 boys; 181 girls
Denomination	Roman Catholic
Fees	No

Pearse College

Address	Clogher Road, Crumlin, Dublin 12
Telephone	01-4536661
Email	information@pearse.cdvec.ie
Principal	E. M. Oxx
School Type	Vocational; Day
Enrolment	248 boys; 292 girls
Denomination	Interdenominational
Fees	No

Rosary College

Address	Armagh Road, Crumlin, Dublin 12
Telephone	01-4555824
Email	rosarycollege.ias@eircom.net
Principal	Brian Maher
School Type	Secondary; Day
Enrolment	21 boys; 178 girls
Denomination	Roman Catholic
Fees	No

St Kevin's College

Address	Clogher Road, Crumlin, Dublin 12
Telephone	01-4536397
Email	info@stkevins.cdvec.ie
Principal	Damien Fee
School Type	Vocational; Day
Enrolment	214 boys; 123 girls
Denomination	Interdenominational
Fees	No

St Paul's Secondary School

Address	Greenhills, Dublin 12
Telephone	01-4505682
Email	info@stpaulsg.ie
Principal	Frances Leahy
School Type	Secondary; Day
Enrolment	762 girls
Denomination	Roman Catholic
Fees	No

Gaelcholáiste Reachrann

Address	Domhnach Mide, Ath Cliath 13
Telephone	01-8770935
Email	fnichaisil@hotmail.com
Principal	Fionnuala Ní Chaisil
School Type	Vocational; Day; All tuition through Irish
Enrolment	94 boys; 63 girls
Denomination	Interdenominational
Fees	No

Grange Community College

Address	Grange Road, Donaghmede, Dublin 13
Telephone	01-8471422
Email	grangeadmin@eircom.net
Principal	Libby Walsh
School Type	Vocational; Day
Enrolment	90 boys; 123 girls
Denomination	Interdenominational
Fees	No

Pobalscoil Neasáin

Address	Baldoyle, Dublin 13
Telephone	01-8063092
Email	pobalscoilneasain@eircom.net
Principal	Mary Carroll
School Type	Community; Day
Enrolment	347 boys; 114 girls
Denomination	Interdenominational
Fees	No

St Dominic's High School

Address	Santa Sabina, Sutton, Dublin 13
Telephone	01-8322200
Email	santasabina@eircom.net
Principal	Nuala Melinn
School Type	Secondary; Day
Enrolment	621 girls
Denomination	Roman Catholic
Fees	No

St Fintan's High School

Address	Dublin Road, Sutton, Dublin 13
Telephone	01-8324632
Email	admin@stfintanshs.ie
Principal	Richard Fogarty
School Type	Secondary; Day
Enrolment	561 boys
Denomination	Roman Catholic
Fees	No

St Mary's Secondary School

Address	Baldoyle, Dublin 13
Telephone	01-8325591
Email	stmbal@indigo.ie
Principal	Sr Elizabeth Slattery
School Type	Secondary; Day
Enrolment	289 girls
Denomination	Roman Catholic
Fees	No

Sutton Park School

Address	St Fintan's Road, Sutton, Dublin 13
Telephone	01-8322940
Email	info@suttonpark.ie
Principal	Raymond Russell
School Type	Secondary; Day & Boarding
Enrolment	168 boys; 121 girls
Denomination	Church of Ireland
Fees	Day Yes Boarding Yes

The Donahies Community School

Address	Streamville Road, Dublin 13
Telephone	01-8473522
Email	donahcs@eircom.net
Principal	Antoinette Ní Gearailt
School Type	Community; Day
Enrolment	281 boys; 267 girls
Denomination	Interdenominational
Fees	No

De La Salle College

Address	Churchtown, Dublin 14
Telephone	01-2981067
Email	dlsctown@iol.ie
Principal	Tim Sheehan
School Type	Secondary; Day
Enrolment	313 boys
Denomination	Roman Catholic
Fees	No

Dundrum College

Address	Sydenham Road, Dundrum, Dublin 14
Telephone	01-2982340
Email	dundrum@iol.ie
Principal	Sean Casey
School Type	Vocational; Day
Enrolment	129 boys; 126 girls
Denomination	Interdenominational
Fees	No

Loreto High School

Address	Beaufort, Grange Road, Rathfarnham, Dublin 14
Telephone	01-4933251
Email	beaufort@eircom.net
Principal	Elizabeth Cogan
School Type	Secondary; Day
Enrolment	612 girls
Denomination	Roman Catholic
Fees	Yes

Mount Anville Secondary School

Address	Mount Anville Road, Dublin 14
Telephone	01-2885313
Email	admin@mountanville.net
Principal	Patricia Bourden
School Type	Secondary; Day
Enrolment	645 girls
Denomination	Roman Catholic
Fees	Yes

Notre Dame Des Missions

Address	Upper Churchtown Road, Dublin 14
Telephone	01-2989533
Email	principal@notredame.ie
Principal	Mildred Brannigan
School Type	Secondary; Day
Enrolment	206 girls
Denomination	Roman Catholic
Fees	Yes

Our Lady's Grove

Address	Goatstown Road, Dublin 14
Telephone	01-2951913
Email	officeolg@eircom.net
Principal	Joyce Kavanagh
School Type	Secondary; Day
Enrolment	433 girls
Denomination	Roman Catholic
Fees	No

St Killian's Deutsche Schule

Address	Roebuck Road, Clonskeagh, Dublin 14
Telephone	01-2883323
Email	admin@killians.com
Principal	Rolf Fenner
School Type	Secondary; Day
Enrolment	128 boys; 128 girls
Denomination	Interdenominational
Fees	Yes

Blakestown Community School

Address	Blanchardstown, Dublin 15
Telephone	01-8215522
Email	admin@blakestowncs.ie
Principal	Victor Black
School Type	Community; Day
Enrolment	265 boys; 275 girls
Denomination	Interdenominational
Fees	No

Castleknock College

Address	Castleknock, Dublin 15	
Telephone	01-8213051	
Email	info@castleknockcollege.ie	
Principal	Andrew McGeady	
School Type	Secondary; Day & Boarding	
Enrolment	575 boys	
Denomination	Roman Catholic	
Fees	Day Yes	Boarding Yes

Castleknock Community College

Address	Carpenterstown Road, Castleknock, Dublin 15
Telephone	01-8221626
Email	admin@castleknockcc.ie
Principal	Thomas O'Brien
School Type	Vocational; Day
Enrolment	581 boys; 563 girls
Denomination	Interdenominational
Fees	No

Hartstown Community School

Address	Hartstown, Clonsilla, Dublin 15
Telephone	01-8207863
Email	hartstowncs@hotmail.com
Principal	Maureen Black
School Type	Community; Day
Enrolment	509 boys; 516 girls
Denomination	Interdenominational
Fees	No

Riversdale Community College

Address	Blanchardstown Road North, Dublin 15
Telephone	01-8201488
Email	rdalecc.ias@eircom.net
Principal	Noel Gildea
School Type	Vocational; Day
Enrolment	233 boys; 219 girls
Denomination	Interdenominational
Fees	No

Scoil Phobail Chuil Mhin

Address	Cluain Saileach, Baile Atha Cliath 15
Telephone	01-8214141
Email	principal@coolminecs.ie
Principal	Eileen Salmon
School Type	Community; Day
Enrolment	574 boys; 538 girls
Denomination	Interdenominational
Fees	No

Ballinteer Community School

Address	Ballinteer, Dublin 16
Telephone	01-2988195
Email	ballcom@eircom.net
Principal	Dr Austin Corcoran
School Type	Community; Day
Enrolment	216 boys; 147 girls
Denomination	Interdenominational
Fees	No

Coláiste Eanna CBS

Address	Ballyroan, Rathfarnham, Dublin 16
Telephone	01-4931767
Email	secretary@colaiste.eanna.ie
Principal	John O'Sullivan
School Type	Secondary; Day
Enrolment	405 boys
Denomination	Roman Catholic
Fees	No

Pobail Scoil Naomh Coilm Cille

Address	Scholarstown Road, Knocklyon, Dublin 16
Telephone	01-4952888
Email	info@knocklyoncs.ie
Principal	John McKennedy
School Type	Community; Day
Enrolment	362 boys; 248 girls
Denomination	Interdenominational
Fees	No

Rockbrook Park School

Address	Edmondstown Road, Rathfarnham, Dublin 16
Telephone	01-4933204
Email	rockbrook@eircom.net
Principal	Joseph M Heneghan
School Type	Secondary; Day
Enrolment	161 boys
Denomination	Roman Catholic
Fees	Yes

St Columba's College

Address	Whitechurch, Dublin 16
Telephone	01-4906791
Email	admin@stcolumbas.ie
Principal	Dr L. J. Haslett
School Type	Secondary; Day & Boarding
Enrolment	168 boys; 127 girls
Denomination	Church of Ireland
Fees	Day Yes Boarding Yes

St Tiernan's Community School

Address	Parkvale, Balally, Dublin 16
Telephone	01-2953224
Email	tiernans@iol.ie
Principal	T. Geraghty
School Type	Community; Day
Enrolment	230 boys; 112 girls
Denomination	Interdenominational
Fees	No

Sancta Maria College

Address	Ballyroan, Rathfarnham, Dublin 16
Telephone	01-4934887
Email	info@sanctamariacollege.com
Principal	Denise Burns
School Type	Secondary; Day
Enrolment	556 girls
Denomination	Roman Catholic
Fees	No

Wesley College

Address	Ballinteer, Dublin 16
Telephone	01-2987066
Email	admin@wesleycollege.ie
Principal	Christopher Woods
School Type	Secondary; Day & Boarding
Enrolment	485 boys; 383 girls
Denomination	Church of Ireland
Fees	Day Yes Boarding Yes

Coláiste Dhúlaigh

Address	Barryscourt Road, Coolock, Dublin 17
Telephone	01-8481337
Email	info@cdc.cdvec.ie
Principal	Seamus Kelly
School Type	Vocational; Day
Enrolment	265 boys; 263 girls
Denomination	Interdenominational
Fees	No

Cabinteely Community School

Address	Cabinteely, Dublin 18
Telephone	01-2852137
Email	ccs@iol.ie
Principal	Joseph Keane
School Type	Community; Day
Enrolment	334 boys; 273 girls
Denomination	Interdenominational
Fees	No

Loreto College

Address	Foxrock, Dublin 18
Telephone	01-2895637
Email	admin@loretofoxrock.ie
Principal	Nuala Mannion
School Type	Secondary; Day
Enrolment	692 girls
Denomination	Roman Catholic
Fees	Yes

St Laurence College

Address	Loughlinstown, Dublin 18
Telephone	01-2826930
Email	info@stlaurencecollege.com
Principal	Michael Redmond
School Type	Secondary; Day
Enrolment	263 boys; 238 girls
Denomination	Roman Catholic
Fees	No

Mount Sackville Secondary School

Address	Chapelizod, Dublin 20
Telephone	01-8213317
Email	info@mountsackville.ie
Principal	Marian McCaughley
School Type	Secondary; Day
Enrolment	630 girls
Denomination	Roman Catholic
Fees	Yes

Pobalscoil Iosolde

Address	Palmerstown, Dublin 20
Telephone	01-6265991
Email	office@pobalscoil-iosolde.ie
Principal	Padraic Gallagher
School Type	Community; Day
Enrolment	235 boys; 182 girls
Denomination	Interdenominational
Fees	No

The King's Hospital

Address	Palmerstown, Dublin 20
Telephone	01-6265933
Email	kingshospitaladmissions@ireland.com
Principal	Frances Hill
School Type	Secondary; Day & Boarding
Enrolment	362 boys; 332 girls
Denomination	Church of Ireland
Fees	Day Yes Boarding Yes

Coláiste Bríde

Address	New Road, Clondalkin, Dublin 22
Telephone	01-4591158
Email	info@colbride.ie
Principal	Marie-Therese Kilmartin
School Type	Secondary; Day
Enrolment	850 girls
Denomination	Roman Catholic
Fees	No

Coláiste Chilliain

Address	Bóthar Nangor, Cluain Dolcain, Baile Atha Cliath 22
Telephone	01-4574888
Email	colchil@indigo.ie
Principal	Seosamh Mac Suibhne
School Type	Vocational; Day; All tuition through Irish
Enrolment	214 boys; 187 girls
Denomination	Interdenominational
Fees	No

Collinstown Park Community College

Address	Neilstown Road, Rowlagh, Clondalkin, Dublin 22
Telephone	01-4572300
Email	admincpcc@eircom.net
Principal	Brian Fleming
School Type	Vocational; Day
Enrolment	278 boys; 359 girls
Denomination	Interdenominational
Fees	No

Deansrath Community College

Address	New Nangor Road, Clondalkin, Dublin 22
Telephone	01-4574144
Email	deansrathcc.ias@eircom.net
Principal	Marie Griffin
School Type	Vocational; Day
Enrolment	205 boys; 242 girls
Denomination	Interdenominational
Fees	No

Moyle Park College

Address	Clondalkin, Dublin 22
Telephone	01-4574837
Email	mpcck@iol.ie
Principal	John Shortt
School Type	Secondary; Day
Enrolment	728 boys
Denomination	Roman Catholic
Fees	No

St Kevin's Community College

Address	Fonthill Road, Clondalkin, Dublin 22
Telephone	01-6266277
Email	stkevinscol@eircom.net
Principal	Paul Duggan
School Type	Vocational; Day
Enrolment	133 boys; 208 girls
Denomination	Interdenominational
Fees	No

Coláiste de hIde

Address	Páirc Thigh Motháin, Tamhlacht, Baile Atha Cliath 24
Telephone	01-4513984
Email	colaistedehide@eircom.net
Principal	Caitlin Mhic Shiacais
School Type	Vocational; Day; All tuition through Irish
Enrolment	115 boys; 124 girls
Denomination	Interdenominational
Fees	No

Firhouse Community College

Address	Firhouse Road, Dublin 24
Telephone	01-4525807
Email	fhsecomd@eircom.net
Principal	Margaret Cavanagh
School Type	Vocational; Day
Enrolment	356 boys; 242 girls
Denomination	Interdenominational
Fees	No

Jobstown Community College

Address	Jobstown, Tallaght, Dublin 24
Telephone	01-4525788
Email	jccschool@eircom.net
Principal	Ronan Connolly
School Type	Vocational; Day
Enrolment	177 boys; 183 girls
Denomination	Interdenominational
Fees	No

Killinarden Community School

Address	Killinarden, Tallaght, Dublin 24
Telephone	01-4527447
Email	ks@iol.ie
Principal	John Fennell
School Type	Community; Day
Enrolment	253 boys; 259 girls
Denomination	Interdenominational
Fees	No

Old Bawn Community School

Address	Old Bawn, Tallaght, Dublin 24
Telephone	01-4520566
Email	obcsdays@eircom.net
Principal	Stiofán Ó Laoire
School Type	Community; Day
Enrolment	427 boys; 355 girls
Denomination	Interdenominational
Fees	No

St Aidan's Community School

Address	Brookfield, Tallaght, Dublin 24
Telephone	01-4524677
Email	sacs@eircom.net
Principal	Michael Meade
School Type	Community; Day
Enrolment	208 boys; 244 girls
Denomination	Interdenominational
Fees	No

St Mark's Community School

Address	Cookstown Road, Tallaght, Dublin 24
Telephone	01-4519399
Email	stmarksoffice@eircom.net
Principal	Irene Kernan
School Type	Community; Day
Enrolment	429 boys; 362 girls
Denomination	Interdenominational
Fees	No

Tallaght Community School

Address	Balrothery, Tallaght, Dublin 24
Telephone	01-4515566
Email	tallaghtcs@eircom.net
Principal	Patrick J. Coffey
School Type	Community; Day
Enrolment	417 boys; 230 girls
Denomination	Interdenominational
Fees	No

Balbriggan Community College

Address	Pine Ridge, Chapel Street, Balbriggan, Co. Dublin
Telephone	01-8412388
Email	shirran@eircom.net
Principal	Pat Halpin
School Type	Vocational; Day
Enrolment	312 boys; 130 girls
Denomination	Interdenominational
Fees	No

Loreto Secondary School

Address	Balbriggan, Co. Dublin
Telephone	01-8411594
Email	lorbal@iol.ie
Principal	Edward Fynes
School Type	Secondary; Day
Enrolment	1052 girls
Denomination	Roman Catholic
Fees	No

Blackrock College

Address	Blackrock, Co. Dublin
Telephone	01-2888681
Email	headmaster@blackrockcollege.com
Principal	Alan McGinty
School Type	Secondary; Day & Boarding
Enrolment	955 boys
Denomination	Roman Catholic
Fees	Day Yes Boarding Yes

CO. DUBLIN

Clonkeen College

Address	Clonkeen Road, Blackrock, Co. Dublin
Telephone	01-2892709
Email	clonkeenrec@eircom.net
Principal	Neil O'Toole
School Type	Secondary; Day
Enrolment	476 boys
Denomination	Roman Catholic
Fees	No

Dominican College

Address	Sion Hill, Blackrock, Co. Dublin
Telephone	01-2886791
Email	admin@sionhillcollege.ie
Principal	Sheila Drumm
School Type	Secondary; Day
Enrolment	261 girls
Denomination	Roman Catholic
Fees	No

Newpark Comprehensive School

Address	Newtown Park Avenue, Blackrock, Co. Dublin
Telephone	01-2883724
Email	newparkoffice@eircom.net
Principal	Derek West
School Type	Comprehensive; Day
Enrolment	491 boys; 307 girls
Denomination	Church of Ireland
Fees	No

Oatlands College

Address	Mount Merrion, Blackrock, Co. Dublin
Telephone	01-2888533
Email	oatlands@iol.ie
Principal	Michael Madigan
School Type	Secondary; Day
Enrolment	366 boys
Denomination	Roman Catholic
Fees	No

Rockford Manor Secondary School

Address	Stradbrook Road, Blackrock, Co. Dublin
Telephone	01-2801522
Email	rockfordadmin@eircom.net
Principal	Rosemary Mitchell
School Type	Secondary; Day
Enrolment	365 girls
Denomination	Roman Catholic
Fees	No

Rosemont School

Address	Temple Road, Blackrock, Co. Dublin
Telephone	01-2833855
Email	info@rosemont.ie
Principal	Marie Farrell
School Type	Secondary; Day
Enrolment	102 girls
Denomination	Roman Catholic
Fees	Yes

St Andrew's College

Address	Booterstown Avenue, Blackrock, Co. Dublin
Telephone	01-2882785
Email	information@st-andrews.ie
Principal	Arthur Godsil
School Type	Secondary; Day
Enrolment	499 boys; 438 girls
Denomination	Church of Ireland
Fees	Yes

St Benildus College

Address	Upper Kilmacud Road, Blackrock, Co. Dublin
Telephone	01-2987836
Email	stbenildus.ias@tinet.ie
Principal	Sean Mulvihill
School Type	Secondary; Day
Enrolment	693 boys
Denomination	Roman Catholic
Fees	No

Willow Park School

Address	Rock Road, Blackrock, Co. Dublin
Telephone	01-2881651
Email	willowadmin@eircom.net
Principal	Donal Brennan
School Type	Secondary; Day & Boarding
Enrolment	196 boys
Denomination	Roman Catholic
Fees	Day Yes Boarding Yes

Loreto Abbey Secondary School

Address	Dalkey, Co. Dublin
Telephone	01-2803061
Email	loreto@clubi.ie
Principal	Dr Dolores McKenna
School Type	Secondary; Day
Enrolment	590 girls
Denomination	Roman Catholic
Fees	Yes

Christian Brothers College

Address	Monkstown Park, Dun Laoghaire, Co. Dublin
Telephone	01-2805854
Email	cbcadmin@indigo.ie
Principal	Patrick Keating
School Type	Secondary; Day
Enrolment	539 boys
Denomination	Roman Catholic
Fees	Yes

Presentation Brothers Glasthule

Address	Glasthule, Dun Laoghaire, Co. Dublin
Telephone	01-2801338
Email	presglasthule@eircom.net
Principal	Jim Murray
School Type	Secondary; Day
Enrolment	101 boys
Denomination	Roman Catholic
Fees	No

Rathdown School

Address	Glenageary, Dun Laoghaire, Co. Dublin
Telephone	01-2853133
Email	principal@rathdownschool.ie
Principal	Barbara Ennis
School Type	Secondary; Day & Boarding
Enrolment	400 girls
Denomination	Church of Ireland
Fees	Day Yes Boarding Yes

Holy Child Secondary School

Address	Military Road, Killiney, Co. Dublin
Telephone	01-2823120
Email	hcsk@eircom.net
Principal	Vera Collins
School Type	Secondary; Day
Enrolment	355 girls
Denomination	Roman Catholic
Fees	Yes

St Joseph of Cluny

Address	Bellevue Park, Ballinclea Road, Killiney, Co. Dublin
Telephone	01-2855027
Email	cluny@eircom.net
Principal	Mary White
School Type	Secondary; Day
Enrolment	452 girls
Denomination	Roman Catholic
Fees	Yes

Coláiste Cois Life

Address	Gleann an Ghrifin, Leamhcan (Lucan), Co. Atha Cliath
Telephone	01-6211825
Email	cclife@indigo.ie
Principal	Aine Ni Ghallchoghair
School Type	Vocational; Day; All tuition through Irish
Enrolment	97 boys; 127 girls
Denomination	Interdenominational
Fees	No

Coláiste Phádraig CBS

Address	Roselawn, Lucan, Co. Dublin
Telephone	01-6282299
Email	colaistelucan@eircom.net
Principal	Brian Murtagh
School Type	Secondary; Day
Enrolment	486 boys; 34 girls
Denomination	Roman Catholic
Fees	No

Lucan Community College

Address	Esker Drive, Lucan, Co. Dublin
Telephone	01-6282077
Email	admin@lucancc.ie
Principal	Séamus O'Neill
School Type	Vocational; Day
Enrolment	443 boys; 381 girls
Denomination	Interdenominational
Fees	No

St Joseph's College

Address	Lucan, Co. Dublin
Telephone	01-6281160
Email	secretary@stjosephslucan.ie
Principal	Siobhán Corry
School Type	Secondary; Day
Enrolment	809 girls
Denomination	Roman Catholic
Fees	No

Malahide Community School

Address	Broomfield, Malahide, Co. Dublin
Telephone	01-8463244
Email	mhidecs@iol.ie
Principal	Brian Cannon
School Type	Community; Day
Enrolment	673 boys; 492 girls
Denomination	Interdenominational
Fees	No

Portmarnock Community School

Address	Carrickhill Road, Portmarnock, Co. Dublin
Telephone	01-8038056
Email	office@portcs.iol.ie
Principal	Pat O'Riordan
School Type	Community; Day
Enrolment	621 boys; 381 girls
Denomination	Interdenominational
Fees	No

Holy Family Community School

Address	Kilteel Road, Rathcoole, Co. Dublin
Telephone	01-4580766
Email	hfcstech@iol.ie
Principal	John G. Walsh
School Type	Community; Day
Enrolment	355 boys; 321 girls
Denomination	Interdenominational
Fees	No

St Joseph's Secondary School

Address	Convent Lane, Rush, Co. Dublin
Telephone	01-8437534
Email	stjrush@iol.ie
Principal	Tom Loughnane
School Type	Secondary; Day
Enrolment	238 boys; 139 girls
Denomination	Roman Catholic
Fees	No

Holy Child Community School

Address	Pearse Street, Sallynoggin, Co. Dublin
Telephone	01-2855334
Email	hccsoff.ias@eircom.net
Principal	Brian McNamara
School Type	Community; Day
Enrolment	125 boys; 161 girls
Denomination	Interdenominational
Fees	No

Skerries Community College

Address	Skerries, Co. Dublin
Telephone	01-8490011
Email	skerriescc@indigo.ie
Principal	Kevin O'Riordan
School Type	Vocational; Day
Enrolment	556 boys; 312 girls
Denomination	Interdenominational
Fees	No

Coláiste Eoin

Address	Bothair Stigh Lorgan (Stillorgan), Co. Atha Cliath
Telephone	01-2884002
Email	coleoin@iol.ie
Principal	Seán Ó Leidhin
School Type	Secondary; Day; All tuition through Irish
Enrolment	421 boys
Denomination	Roman Catholic
Fees	No

Coláiste Iosagáin

Address	Bóthar Stigh Lorgan (Stillorgan), Co. Atha Cliath
Telephone	01-2884028
Email	iosagain.ias@eircom.net
Principal	Maedhbh Uí Chiagain
School Type	Secondary; Day; All tuition through Irish
Enrolment	462 girls
Denomination	Roman Catholic
Fees	No

St Raphaela's Secondary School

Address	Upper Kilmacud Road, Stillorgan, Co. Dublin
Telephone	01-2888730
Email	straphaelas@eircom.net
Principal	Eileen O'Donnell
School Type	Secondary; Day
Enrolment	420 girls
Denomination	Roman Catholic
Fees	No

Coláiste Choilm

Address	Dublin Road, Swords, Co. Dublin
Telephone	01-8401420
Email	colchoilm.ias@eircom.net
Principal	Sharon Costello
School Type	Secondary; Day
Enrolment	603 boys
Denomination	Roman Catholic
Fees	No

Fingal Community College

Address	Seatown Road, Swords, Co. Dublin
Telephone	01-8405829
Email	fingalcc1@eircom.net
Principal	Tony Keeling
School Type	Vocational; Day
Enrolment	270 boys; 261 girls
Denomination	Interdenominational
Fees	No

Loreto College

Address	Swords, Co. Dublin
Telephone	01-8407025
Email	lorsword@iol.ie
Principal	Veronica McDermott
School Type	Secondary; Day
Enrolment	631 girls
Denomination	Roman Catholic
Fees	No

St Finian's Community College

Address	Swords, Co. Dublin
Telephone	01-8402623
Email	stfinians.ias@eircom.net
Principal	Shaun Purcell
School Type	Vocational; Day
Enrolment	323 boys; 285 girls
Denomination	Interdenominational
Fees	No

GALWAY

Coláiste Einde

Address	Threadneedle Road, Galway
Telephone	091-521407
Email	colaisteeinde@eircom.net
Principal	Siobhan Quinn
School Type	Secondary; Day
Enrolment	347 boys; 206 girls
Denomination	Roman Catholic
Fees	No

Coláiste na Coiribe

Address	Bothar Thuama, Gaillimh
Telephone	091-753977
Email	colaistenacoiribe@eircom.net
Principal	Tomás Mac Pháidín
School Type	Vocational; Day; All tuition through Irish
Enrolment	92 boys; 103 girls
Denomination	Interdenominational
Fees	No

Dominican College

Address	Taylors Hill, Galway
Telephone	091-523171
Email	taylors@vol.ie
Principal	Eilish Keaveney
School Type	Secondary; Day
Enrolment	648 girls
Denomination	Roman Catholic
Fees	No

Galway Community College

Address	Wellpark, Galway
Telephone	091-755464
Email	tyrellc@galwaycc.iol.ie
Principal	Christy Tyrrell
School Type	Vocational; Day
Enrolment	329 boys; 259 girls
Denomination	Interdenominational
Fees	No

Galway Technical Institute

Address	Father Griffin Road, Galway
Telephone	091-581342
Email	peter.keady@cgvec.ie
Principal	Peter Keady
School Type	Vocational; Day
Enrolment	265 boys; 527 girls
Denomination	Interdenominational
Fees	No

Jesus & Mary Secondary School

Address	Salerno, Threadneedle Road, Salthill, Galway
Telephone	091-529500
Email	salernoadmin@eircom.net
Principal	Sr Gerarda Lawler
School Type	Secondary; Day
Enrolment	478 girls
Denomination	Roman Catholic
Fees	No

Mercy Secondary School

Address	Newtownsmith, Galway
Telephone	091-566595
Email	msm@eircom.net
Principal	Dr Brendan Lydon
School Type	Secondary; Day
Enrolment	360 girls
Denomination	Roman Catholic
Fees	No

Presentation Secondary School

Address	Presentation Road, Galway
Telephone	091-563495
Email	presgalpdp@eircom.net
Principal	Michael McCann
School Type	Secondary; Day
Enrolment	327 girls
Denomination	Roman Catholic
Fees	No

St Joseph's College

Address	Nun's Island, Galway
Telephone	091-565980
Email	admin@bish.ie
Principal	Peadar Ó hIci
School Type	Secondary; Day
Enrolment	784 boys
Denomination	Roman Catholic
Fees	No

St Mary's College

Address	St Mary's Road, Galway
Telephone	091-522369
Email	smcollege@eircom.net
Principal	Bartley Fannin
School Type	Secondary; Day
Enrolment	550 boys
Denomination	Roman Catholic
Fees	No

Scoil Chuimsitheach Chiaráin

Address	An Cheathrú Rua, Co. na Gaillimhe
Telephone	091-595215
Email	scoilcc@eircom.ie
Principal	Máire de Bhaldraithe
School Type	Comprehensive; Day; All tuition through Irish
Enrolment	177 boys; 184 girls
Denomination	Interdenominational
Fees	No

Coláiste Chroí Mhuire

Address	An Spideal, Co. na Gaillimhe
Telephone	091-553113
Email	ccmspideal@hotmail.com
Principal	Tríona Uí Mhurchú
School Type	Secondary; Day; All tuition through Irish
Enrolment	192 boys; 170 girls
Denomination	Roman Catholic
Fees	No

CO. GALWAY

Gairmscoil Einne Oileáin Arann

Address	Cill Rónain, Inis Mór, Arainn, Co. na Gaillimhe
Telephone	099-61184
Email	gseinne.ias@eircom.net
Principal	Micheál Ó Goill
School Type	Vocational; Day; All tuition through Irish
Enrolment	28 boys; 32 girls
Denomination	Interdenominational
Fees	No

Gairmscoil Mhuire

Address	Athenry, Co. Galway
Telephone	091-844159
Email	athenryvocschool@eircom.net
Principal	Malachy Naughton
School Type	Vocational; Day
Enrolment	391 boys; 236 girls
Denomination	Interdenominational
Fees	No

Presentation College

Address	Athenry, Co. Galway
Telephone	091-844144
Email	pcathenry@hotmail.com
Principal	Mary Forde
School Type	Secondary; Day
Enrolment	263 boys; 299 girls
Denomination	Roman Catholic
Fees	No

Gairmscoil Chilleáin Naofa

Address	Cnoc Breac, New Inn, Ballinasloe, Co. Galway
Telephone	090-9675811
Email	stkilliansvs.ias@eircom.net
Principal	Thomas Mac Lochlainn
School Type	Vocational; Day
Enrolment	111 boys; 95 girls
Denomination	Interdenominational
Fees	No

Scoil Mhuire

Address	Society Street, Ballinasloe, Co. Galway
Telephone	090-9642206
Email	ardscoilmhuire@eircom.net
Principal	Mary Molloy
School Type	Secondary; Day
Enrolment	457 girls
Denomination	Roman Catholic
Fees	No

St Cuan's College

Address	Castleblakney, Ballinasloe, Co. Galway
Telephone	090-9678127
Email	saintcuana@eircom.net
Principal	Eamonn O'Donoghue
School Type	Secondary; Day
Enrolment	86 boys; 121 girls
Denomination	Roman Catholic
Fees	No

St Jarlath's Vocational School

Address	Mountbellew, Ballinasloe, Co. Galway
Telephone	090-9679231
Email	mountbellewvs@eircom.net
Principal	Matthew Kilroy
School Type	Vocational; Day
Enrolment	75 boys; 30 girls
Denomination	Interdenominational
Fees	No

Coláiste Mhuire

Address	Ballygar, Co. Galway
Telephone	090-6624740
Email	smcballygar@eircom.net
Principal	Patrick McDonagh
School Type	Secondary; Day
Enrolment	165 boys; 143 girls
Denomination	Roman Catholic
Fees	No

Coláiste Sheosaimh

Address	Gearrbhaile, Beál Ath na Slua, Co. na Gaillimhe
Telephone	090-9642504
Email	garbally@iol.ie
Principal	Thomas Blanche
School Type	Secondary; Day & Boarding
Enrolment	541 boys
Denomination	Roman Catholic
Fees	Day No Boarding Yes

Coláiste Iognáid SJ

Address	Bóthar na Mara, Gaillimh
Telephone	091-501550
Email	iognaid@iol.ie
Principal	Padhraic Lydon
School Type	Secondary; Day; At least one subject other than Irish taught through Irish
Enrolment	335 boys; 278 girls
Denomination	Roman Catholic
Fees	No

Scoil Phobail Mhic Dara

Address	Carna, Co. na Gaillimhe
Telephone	095-32245
Email	spmd@eircom.net
Principal	Tomás O Nidh
School Type	Community; Day; All tuition through Irish
Enrolment	104 boys; 99 girls
Denomination	Interdenominational
Fees	No

Scoil Phobail

Address	Clifden, Co. Galway
Telephone	095-21184
Email	clifden@iol.ie
Principal	Br James Mungovan
School Type	Community; Day
Enrolment	225 boys; 194 girls
Denomination	Interdenominational
Fees	No

Kylemore Abbey School

Address	Connemara, Co. Galway
Telephone	095-41444
Email	principal@kylemoreabbey.ie
Principal	Mary Dempsey
School Type	Secondary; Day & Boarding
Enrolment	137 girls
Denomination	Roman Catholic
Fees	Day No Boarding Yes

Gairmscoil Fheichin Naofa

Address	Corr na Mona, Co. na Gaillimhe
Telephone	092-48006
Email	corrvec@eircom.net
Principal	Brian Ó Maoilchiaráin
School Type	Vocational; Day; All tuition through Irish
Enrolment	49 boys; 35 girls
Denomination	Interdenominational
Fees	No

Dunmore Community School

Address	Dunmore, Co. Galway
Telephone	093-38203
Email	dunmorecs@eircom.net
Principal	Patrick Gilmore
School Type	Community; Day
Enrolment	191 boys; 265 girls
Denomination	Interdenominational
Fees	No

Glenamaddy Community School

Address	Glenamaddy, Co. Galway
Telephone	094-9659315
Email	glenamaddycs@eircom.net
Principal	James Duignan
School Type	Community; Day
Enrolment	157 boys; 241 girls
Denomination	Interdenominational
Fees	No

Gort Community School

Address	Gort, Co. Galway
Telephone	091-632163
Email	gortcomm@iol.ie
Principal	Denis A. Corry
School Type	Community; Day
Enrolment	414 boys; 246 girls
Denomination	Interdenominational
Fees	No

Presentation College

Address	Headford, Co. Galway
Telephone	093-35408
Email	prescollhead@eircom.net
Principal	James Whyte
School Type	Secondary; Day
Enrolment	330 boys; 342 girls
Denomination	Roman Catholic
Fees	No

Coláiste Cholmcille

Address	Indreabhán, Co. na Gaillimhe
Telephone	091-593119
Email	cccille@eircom.net
Principal	Tomás Mac Gloinn
School Type	Vocational; Day; All tuition through Irish
Enrolment	103 boys; 106 girls
Denomination	Interdenominational
Fees	No

Seamount College

Address	Kinvara, Co. Galway
Telephone	091-637362
Email	seamount.ias@eircom.net
Principal	Eileen Mulkerrins
School Type	Secondary; Day
Enrolment	233 girls
Denomination	Roman Catholic
Fees	No

St Brigid's Vocational School

Address	Loughrea, Co. Galway
Telephone	091-841919
Email	stbrigidsvec@eircom.net
Principal	Michael Bond
School Type	Vocational; Day
Enrolment	283 boys; 340 girls
Denomination	Interdenominational
Fees	No

St Raphael's College

Address	Loughrea, Co. Galway
Telephone	091-841062
Email	straphaelsloughrea@eircom.net
Principal	Margaret Burke
School Type	Secondary; Day
Enrolment	128 boys; 172 girls
Denomination	Roman Catholic
Fees	No

Holy Rosary College

Address	Mountbellew, Co. Galway
Telephone	090-9679222
Email	info@hrc.ie
Principal	John Fahey
School Type	Secondary; Day
Enrolment	229 boys; 278 girls
Denomination	Roman Catholic
Fees	No

Coláiste Ghobnait

Address	Inis Oirr, Oileain Arann, Cuan na Gaillimhe
Telephone	099-75016
Email	colaisteghobnait@eircom.net
Principal	Brid Uí Dhonncha
School Type	Vocational; Day; All tuition through Irish
Enrolment	16 boys; 8 girls
Denomination	Interdenominational
Fees	No

Calasanctius College

Address	Oranmore, Co. Galway
Telephone	091-794564
Email	ehannon@calasanctius.ie
Principal	Elizabeth Hannon
School Type	Secondary; Day
Enrolment	315 boys; 343 girls
Denomination	Roman Catholic
Fees	No

St Paul's

Address	Oughterard, Co. Galway
Telephone	091-552689
Email	naomhpol@iol.ie
Principal	Mary Nihill
School Type	Secondary; Day
Enrolment	196 boys; 208 girls
Denomination	Roman Catholic
Fees	No

Portumna Community School

Address	Portumna, Co. Galway
Telephone	090-9741053
Email	principal@portumnacs.com
Principal	David Leahy
School Type	Community; Day
Enrolment	217 boys; 242 girls
Denomination	Interdenominational
Fees	No

Gairmscoil na bPiarsach

Address	Ros Muc, Co. na Gaillimhe
Telephone	091-574100
Email	piarsach@eircom.net
Principal	Máire Áine Uí Chatháin
School Type	Vocational; Day; All tuition through Irish
Enrolment	29 boys; 22 girls
Denomination	Interdenominational
Fees	No

Presentation College

Address	Currylea, Tuam, Co. Galway
Telephone	093-24575
Email	prescurrylea@eircom.net
Principal	Tony Lillis
School Type	Secondary; Day
Enrolment	440 girls
Denomination	Roman Catholic
Fees	No

St Brigid's School

Address	Convent of Mercy, Tuam, Co. Galway
Telephone	093-24199
Email	stbrigidstuam.ias@eircom.net
Principal	John G. Davin
School Type	Secondary; Day
Enrolment	316 girls
Denomination	Roman Catholic
Fees	No

St Jarlath's College

Address	Tuam, Co. Galway
Telephone	093-24342
Email	info@jarlaths.ie
Principal	Fr Conal Eustace
School Type	Secondary; Day & Boarding
Enrolment	416 boys
Denomination	Roman Catholic
Fees	Day No Boarding Yes

St Patrick's College

Address	Dublin Road, Tuam, Co. Galway
Telephone	093-28319
Email	principalstpats@eircom.net
Principal	Kevin O'Dwyer
School Type	Secondary; Day
Enrolment	260 boys
Denomination	Roman Catholic
Fees	No

Archbishop McHale College

Address	Tuam, Co. Galway
Telephone	093-24237
Email	amctuam@eircom.net
Principal	Eileen Delaney
School Type	Vocational; Day
Enrolment	66 boys; 63 girls
Denomination	Interdenominational
Fees	No

Mercy College

Address	Woodford, Co. Galway
Telephone	090-9749076
Email	admin@mercycollegewoodford.com
Principal	Frances Holohan
School Type	Secondary; Day
Enrolment	117 boys; 139 girls
Denomination	Roman Catholic
Fees	No

St Joseph's Secondary School

Address	Ballybunion, Co. Kerry
Telephone	068-27205
Email	sjsb@ireland.com
Principal	John Atkinson
School Type	Secondary; Day
Enrolment	80 boys; 82 girls
Denomination	Roman Catholic
Fees	No

Coláiste na Sceilge

Address	Caherciveen, Co. Kerry
Telephone	066-9473335
Email	coláistenasceilge@hotmail.com
Principal	Michael Donnelly
School Type	Vocational; Day; One stream has all tuition through Irish
Enrolment	294 boys; 303 girls
Denomination	Interdenominational
Fees	No

CO. KERRY

Castleisland Community College

Address	Tonbwee, Castleisland, Co. Kerry
Telephone	066-7141196
Email	castleccadmin@eircom.net
Principal	Anne O'Sullivan
School Type	Vocational; Day
Enrolment	178 boys; 94 girls
Denomination	Interdenominational
Fees	No

Meán Scoil Naomh Ioseph

Address	Clochar na Toirbhirte, Castleisland, Co. Kerry
Telephone	066-7141178
Email	presconvent.ias@eircom.net
Principal	Seamus Falvey
School Type	Secondary; Day
Enrolment	226 girls
Denomination	Roman Catholic
Fees	No

Coláiste Bhréanainn

Address	Cill Airne, Co. Chiarraí
Telephone	064-31021
Email	stbrendkill@eircom.net
Principal	Ed O'Neill
School Type	Secondary; Day
Enrolment	464 boys; 11 girls
Denomination	Roman Catholic
Fees	No

Coláiste Íde

Address	Baile an Ghóilín, Daingean Uí Chuis, Co. Chiarraí
Telephone	066-9151211
Email	info@colaisteide.com
Principal	Máire Uí Mhurchú
School Type	Secondary; Boarding only; All tuition through Irish
Enrolment	75 girls
Denomination	Roman Catholic
Fees	Yes

Meán Scoil na mBráithre Críostaí

Address	Daingean Uí Chúis, Co. Chiarraí
Telephone	066-9151853
Email	pfcbs.ias@eircom.net
Principal	Padraig Firtear
School Type	Secondary; Day; All tuition through Irish
Enrolment	258 boys
Denomination	Roman Catholic
Fees	No

Meánscoil na Toirbhirte

Address	Daingean Uí Chúis, Co. Chiarraí
Telephone	066-9151605
Email	tomcrowley@eircom.ie
Principal	Tomás Ó Cruadhlaoich
School Type	Secondary; Day; All tuition through Irish
Enrolment	270 girls
Denomination	Roman Catholic
Fees	No

Pobalscoil Inbhear Scéine

Address	Kenmare, Co. Kerry
Telephone	064-40846
Email	info@kenmarecs.com
Principal	Dermot Healy
School Type	Community; Day
Enrolment	242 boys; 203 girls
Denomination	Interdenominational
Fees	No

Killarney Community College

Address	New Road, Killarney, Co. Kerry
Telephone	064-32164
Email	kcccom@iol.ie
Principal	Pat Favier
School Type	Vocational; Day
Enrolment	138 boys; 130 girls
Denomination	Interdenominational
Fees	No

Presentation Secondary School

Address	Miltown, Killarney, Co. Kerry
Telephone	066-9767168
Email	miltownpres3@eircom.net
Principal	Sr Canisius
School Type	Secondary; Day
Enrolment	220 boys; 250 girls
Denomination	Roman Catholic
Fees	No

St Brigid's Secondary School

Address	New Street, Killarney, Co. Kerry
Telephone	064-32209
Email	prstbrigidsc@eircom.net
Principal	Margaret MacCormack
School Type	Secondary; Day
Enrolment	403 girls
Denomination	Roman Catholic
Fees	No

Community College

Address	Killorglin, Co. Kerry
Telephone	066-9761168
Email	killorglincc@eircom.net
Principal	Austin O'Reilly
School Type	Vocational; Day
Enrolment	81 boys; 74 girls
Denomination	Interdenominational
Fees	No

The Intermediate School

Address	Iveragh Road, Killorglin, Co. Kerry
Telephone	066-9761246
Email	iskadmins@eircom.net
Principal	Kieran Griffin
School Type	Secondary; Day
Enrolment	358 boys; 382 girls
Denomination	Roman Catholic
Fees	No

Listowel Community College

Address	Listowel, Co. Kerry
Telephone	068-21023
Email	lccadmin@eircom.net
Principal	Seán MacCarthy
School Type	Vocational; Day
Enrolment	49 boys; 102 girls
Denomination	Interdenominational
Fees	No

Comprehensive School

Address	Tarbert, Listowel, Co. Kerry
Telephone	068-36105
Email	tarbert@iol.ie
Principal	Mary McGillicuddy
School Type	Comprehensive; Day
Enrolment	367 boys; 263 girls
Denomination	Interdenominational
Fees	No

Presentation Secondary School

Address	Listowel, Co. Kerry
Telephone	068-21452
Email	pressec@indigo.ie
Principal	Sr Nuala O'Leary
School Type	Secondary; Day
Enrolment	416 girls
Denomination	Roman Catholic
Fees	No

St Michael's College

Address	Listowel, Co. Kerry
Telephone	068-21049
Email	smc.ias@eircom.net
Principal	John Mulvihill
School Type	Secondary; Day
Enrolment	229 boys
Denomination	Roman Catholic
Fees	No

Scoil Phobail Sliabh Luachra

Address	Rathmore, Co. Kerry
Telephone	064-58135
Email	rathmorecs@eircom.net
Principal	Jeremiah O'Donoghue
School Type	Community; Day
Enrolment	Boys 228; 229 girls
Denomination	Interdenominational
Fees	No

Causeway Comprehensive School

Address	Causeway, Tralee, Co. Kerry
Telephone	066-7131197
Email	causewaycs@eircom.net
Principal	John O'Regan
School Type	Comprehensive; Day
Enrolment	233 boys; 225 girls
Denomination	Interdenominational
Fees	No

CBS Secondary School

Address	The Green, Tralee, Co. Kerry
Telephone	066-7145824
Email	tonyok@eircom.net
Principal	Anthony O'Keeffe
School Type	Secondary; Day
Enrolment	660 boys
Denomination	Roman Catholic
Fees	No

Mercy Secondary School

Address	Mounthawk, Tralee, Co. Kerry
Telephone	066-7102550
Email	admin@mercymounthawk.ie
Principal	Tony Behan
School Type	Secondary; Day
Enrolment	489 boys; 633 girls
Denomination	Roman Catholic
Fees	No

Presentation Secondary School

Address	Tralee, Co. Kerry
Telephone	066-7122737
Email	prestralee@eircom.net
Principal	Sr Brid Clifford
School Type	Secondary; Day
Enrolment	663 girls
Denomination	Roman Catholic
Fees	No

Tralee Community College

Address	Clash, Tralee, Co. Kerry
Telephone	066-7121741
Email	tccoffice@eircom.net
Principal	Billy Curtin
School Type	Vocational; Day
Enrolment	203 boys; 199 girls
Denomination	Interdenominational
Fees	No

Gaelcholáiste Chiarraí

Address	Tobar Mhaigh Dor, Trá Lí, Co. Chiarraí
Telephone	066-7121650
Email	gaelcholaiste.ias@eircom.net
Principal	Padraig Ó Dálaigh
School Type	Vocational; Day; All tuition through Irish
Enrolment	101 boys; 104 girls
Denomination	Interdenominational
Fees	No

Meánscoil an Leith-Triúigh

Address	Bréanann, Trá Lí, Co. Chiarraí
Telephone	066-7139746
Principal	Ciarán Ó Beaglaoich
School Type	Secondary; Day; At least one subject other than Irish taught through Irish
Enrolment	33 boys; 31 girls
Denomination	Roman Catholic
Fees	No

CO. KILDARE

Athy Community College

Address	Athy, Co. Kildare
Telephone	059-8631663
Email	rdaly@athycollege.ie
Principal	Richard Daly
School Type	Vocational; Day
Enrolment	104 boys; 148 girls
Denomination	Interdenominatinal
Fees	No

Scoil Eoin

Address	Rathstewart, Athy, Co. Kildare
Telephone	059-8638223
Email	scoileoin.ias@tinet.ie
Principal	Tony O'Rourke
School Type	Secondary; Day
Enrolment	302 boys
Denomination	Roman Catholic
Fees	No

Scoil Mhuire

Address	Rathstewart, Athy, Co. Kildare
Telephone	059-8638215
Email	scmhuire@eircom.net
Principal	Damien Kennedy
School Type	Secondary; Day
Enrolment	299 girls
Denomination	Roman Catholic
Fees	No

Coláiste Lorcáin

Address	Castledermot, Co. Kildare
Telephone	059-9144167
Email	principal@colaistelorcain.com
Principal	Michael Russell
School Type	Vocational; Day
Enrolment	156 boys; 171 girls
Denomination	Interdenominational
Fees	No

St Wolstan's Community School

Address	Ballymakeely, Clane Road, Celbridge, Co. Kildare
Telephone	01-6288257
Email	info@stwolstans.net
Principal	Maria Barry
School Type	Community; Day
Enrolment	748 girls
Denomination	Interdenominational
Fees	No

Salesian College

Address	Celbridge, Co. Kildare
Telephone	01-6272166
Email	salcol@eircom.net
Principal	Fr Daniel Carroll
School Type	Secondary; Day
Enrolment	684 boys
Denomination	Roman Catholic
Fees	No

Curragh Post-Primary School

Address	McSwiney Road, Curragh, Co. Kildare
Telephone	045-441809
Email	principal@curragh.org
Principal	Brian Donohue
School Type	Vocational; Day
Enrolment	74 boys; 105 girls
Denomination	Interdenominational
Fees	No

Gael Choláiste Chill Dara

Address	An Bothar Glas, An Currach (Curragh), Co. Chill Dara
Telephone	045-441797
Email	gchcd@eircom.net
Principal	Séamus Ó Ceanainn
School Type	Secondary; Day; All tuition through Irish
Enrolment	18 boys; 16 girls
Denomination	Roman Catholic
Fees	No

Scoil Dara

Address	Church Street, Kilcock, Co. Kildare
Telephone	01-6287258
Email	scoildara@eircom.net
Principal	P J Gannon
School Type	Secondary; Day
Enrolment	383 boys; 377 girls
Denomination	Roman Catholic
Fees	No

Cross and Passion College

Address	Kilcullen, Co. Kildare
Telephone	045-481524
Email	cpc.ias@eircom.net
Principal	Paul P Tyrell
School Type	Secondary; Day
Enrolment	295 boys; 340 girls
Denomination	Roman Catholic
Fees	No

Presentation Secondary School

Address	Kildare Town, Co. Kildare
Telephone	045-521654
Email	psskprincipal@eircom.net
Principal	Herbert Williams
School Type	Secondary; Day
Enrolment	203 girls
Denomination	Roman Catholic
Fees	No

St Joseph's Academy

Address	Kildare Town, Co. Kildare
Telephone	045-521788
Email	stjosephsacademy@eircom.net
Principal	Eamonn Mulvihill
School Type	Secondary; Day
Enrolment	191 boys
Denomination	Roman Catholic
Fees	No

Kildare Vocational School

Address	Kildare Town, Co. Kildare
Telephone	045-521287
Email	michaelbyrneskildarevec@eircom.net
Principal	Michael Byrnes
School Type	Vocational; Day
Enrolment	27 boys; 38 girls
Denomination	Interdenominational
Fees	No

Confey Community College

Address	Confey, Leixlip, Co. Kildare
Telephone	01-6245322
Email	info@confeycollege.org
Principal	Cathal Travers
School Type	Vocational; Day
Enrolment	288 boys; 330 girls
Denomination	Interdenominational
Fees	No

Coláiste Chiaráin

Address	Celbridge Road, Leixlip, Co. Kildare
Telephone	01-6243226
Email	jsprincipal@eircom.net
Principal	Joseph Sweeney
School Type	Community; Day
Enrolment	340 boys; 273 girls
Denomination	Interdenominational
Fees	No

Maynooth Post-Primary School

Address	Moyglare Road, Maynooth, Co. Kildare
Telephone	01-6286060
Email	principal@mpps.ie
Principal	Senan Griffin
School Type	Vocational; Day
Enrolment	423 boys; 397 girls
Denomination	Interdenominational
Fees	No

St Paul's Secondary School

Address	Monasterevin, Co. Kildare
Telephone	045-525601
Email	stpaulssec@tinet.ie
Principal	Derek Egan
School Type	Secondary; Day
Enrolment	104 boys; 101 girls
Denomination	Roman Catholic
Fees	No

Meánscoil Iognáid Ris

Address	Naas, Co. Kildare
Telephone	045-866402
Email	admin@naascbs.ie
Principal	Noel Merrick
School Type	Secondary; Day
Enrolment	772 boys
Denomination	Roman Catholic
Fees	No

Clongowes Wood College

Address	Naas, Co. Kildare
Telephone	045-868202
Email	hm@clongowes.ie
Principal	Fr Leonard Moloney, SJ
School Type	Secondary; Boarding only
Enrolment	447 boys
Denomination	Roman Catholic
Fees	Yes

Coláiste Naomh Mhuire

Address	Convent of Mercy, Naas, Co. Kildare
Telephone	045-879634
Email	smcnaas@eircom.net
Principal	Marie O'Neill
School Type	Secondary; Day
Enrolment	806 girls
Denomination	Roman Catholic
Fees	No

St Farnan's Post-Primary School

Address	Prosperous, Naas, Co. Kildare
Telephone	045-868152
Email	stfarnan@iol.ie
Principal	Patricia O'Brien
School Type	Vocational; Day
Enrolment	144 boys; 184 girls
Denomination	Interdenominational
Fees	No

St Patrick's Community College

Address	Old Newbridge Road, Naas, Co. Kildare
Telephone	045-897885
Email	principalncc@eircom.net
Principal	Colm O'Connor
School Type	Vocational; Day
Enrolment	150 boys; 186 girls
Denomination	Interdenominational
Fees	No

Scoil Mhuire Community School

Address	Clane, Naas, Co. Kildare
Telephone	045-868121
Email	Scoilmhuire.clane@gmail.com
Principal	Sr Dominica Murphy
School Type	Community; Day
Enrolment	335 boys; 370 girls
Denomination	Interdenominational
Fees	No

Holy Family Secondary School

Address	Newbridge, Co. Kildare
Telephone	045-431957
Email	hfss.ias@eircom.net
Principal	Patricia O'Callaghan
School Type	Secondary; Day
Enrolment	627 girls
Denomination	Roman Catholic
Fees	No

Newbridge College

Address	Newbridge, Co. Kildare
Telephone	045-487200
Email	info@newbridge-college.ie
Principal	Patrick J O'Mahony
School Type	Secondary; Day
Enrolment	395 boys; 348 girls
Denomination	Roman Catholic
Fees	Yes

Patrician Secondary School

Address	Newbridge, Co. Kildare
Telephone	045-432410
Email	pbsnbridge@tinet.ie
Principal	Peter O'Reilly
School Type	Secondary; Day
Enrolment	630 boys
Denomination	Roman Catholic
Fees	No

St Conleth's Vocational School

Address	Station Road, Newbridge, Co. Kildare
Telephone	045-431417
Email	stconlethsvs@eircom.net
Principal	Brendan Dunning
School Type	Vocational; Day
Enrolment	146 boys; 201 girls
Denomination	Interdenominational
Fees	No

Ardscoil Rath Iomgháin

Address	Rathangan, Co. Kildare
Telephone	045-524384
Email	ardsri@iol.ie
Principal	Stephen Hartnett
School Type	Vocational; Day
Enrolment	238 boys; 206 girls
Denomination	Interdenominational
Fees	No

Scoil Aireagail

Address	Ballyhale, Co. Kilkenny
Telephone	056-7768632
Email	scoilaireagail@eircom.net
Principal	Thomas A. Hunt
School Type	Vocational; Day
Enrolment	205 boys; 155 girls
Denomination	Interdenominational
Fees	No

Coláiste Eamann Rís

Address	Callan, Co. Kilkenny
Telephone	056-7725340
Email	coleamannris.ias@eircom.ie
Principal	Donal O'Hanlon
School Type	Secondary; Day
Enrolment	206 boys
Denomination	Roman Catholic
Fees	No

St Brigid's College

Address	Callan, Co. Kilkenny	
Telephone	056-7725189	
Email	colbrid@iol.ie	
Principal	Patrick Power	
School Type	Secondary; Day & Boarding	
Enrolment	440 girls	
Denomination	Roman Catholic	
Fees	Day No	Boarding Yes

Castlecomer Community School

Address	Castlecomer, Co. Kilkenny
Telephone	056-4441447
Email	commoffi@iol.ie
Principal	Seamus O'Connor
School Type	Community; Day
Enrolment	312 boys; 332 girls
Denomination	Interdenominational
Fees	No

CO. KILKENNY

Meánscoil na mBráithre Criostaí

Address	Sráid Shéamais, Cill Channaigh
Telephone	056-21402
Email	cbskk@indigo.ie
Principal	Dermot P Curran
School Type	Secondary; Day
Enrolment	635 boys
Denomination	Roman Catholic
Fees	No

Dúiske College

Address	Graignamanagh, Co. Kilkenny
Telephone	059-9724177
Email	duiskeadmin@eircom.net
Principal	Séamus Knox
School Type	Vocational; Day
Enrolment	51 boys; 75 girls
Denomination	Interdenominational
Fees	No

Coláiste Mhuire

Address	Johnstown, Co. Kilkenny
Telephone	056-8831135
Email	kkmhuire@eircom.net
Principal	John Cahill
School Type	Vocational; Day
Enrolment	208 boys; 186 girls
Denomination	Interdenominational
Fees	No

City Vocational School

Address	New Street, Kilkenny, Co. Kilkenny
Telephone	056-7722108
Email	kcvsoffice@eircom.net
Principal	Cathy McSorley
School Type	Vocational; Day; One stream has all tuition through Irish
Enrolment	146 boys; 174 girls
Denomination	Interdenominational
Fees	No

Kilkenny College

Address	Castlecomer Road, Kilkenny, Co. Kilkenny
Telephone	056-7761544
Email	kck@indigo.ie
Principal	Canon Robert J Black
School Type	Secondary; Day & Boarding;
Enrolment	430 boys; 358 girls
Denomination	Church of Ireland
Fees	Day Yes Boarding Yes

Loreto Secondary School

Address	Granges Road, Kilkenny, Co. Kilkenny
Telephone	056-7765132
Email	principal@loretokk.ie
Principal	Helen Renehan
School Type	Secondary; Day
Enrolment	786 girls
Denomination	Roman Catholic
Fees	No

St Kieran's College

Address	College Road, Kilkenny, Co. Kilkenny
Telephone	056-7761707
Email	stkieransadmin@eircom.net
Principal	Michael Ó Diarmada
School Type	Secondary; Day & Boarding
Enrolment	632 boys
Denomination	Roman Catholic
Fees	Day No Boarding Yes

Presentation Secondary School

Address	Loughboy, Kilkenny, Co. Kilkenny
Telephone	056-7765684
Email	preskilkenny@eircom.net
Principal	Cathal Cullen
School Type	Secondary; Day
Enrolment	575 girls
Denomination	Roman Catholic
Fees	No

Coláiste Cois Siúire

Address	Mooncoin, Co. Kilkenny
Telephone	051-895112
Email	colcoissiuire@eircom.net
Principal	Thomas Walsh
School Type	Vocational; Day
Enrolment	133 boys; 93 girls
Denomination	Interdenominational
Fees	No

Grennan College

Address	Ladywell Street, Thomastown, Co. Kilkenny
Telephone	056-7724112
Email	grennancollege@eircom.net
Principal	William P. Norton
School Type	Vocational; Day
Enrolment	155 boys; 193 girls
Denomination	Interdenominational
Fees	No

Heywood Community School

Address	Ballinakill, Co. Laois
Telephone	057-8733333
Email	90hwood@eircom.net
Principal	David Dwyer
School Type	Community; Day
Enrolment	346 boys; 313 girls
Denomination	Interdenominational
Fees	No

Clonaslee Vocational School

Address	Clonaslee, Co. Laois
Telephone	0502-48044
Email	clonvs.ias@tinet.ie
Principal	Fran Bates
School Type	Vocational; Day
Enrolment	79 boys; 106 girls
Denomination	Interdenominational
Fees	No

Community School

Address	Mountmellick, Co. Laois
Telephone	0502-24220
Email	mountmellickcs.ias@eircom.net
Principal	Eric Gaughran
School Type	Community; Day
Enrolment	287 boys; 222 girls
Denomination	Interdenominational
Fees	No

Brigidine Secondary School

Address	Mountrath, Co. Laois
Telephone	0502-32613
Email	bssmt@iol.ie
Principal	Mary Kavanagh
School Type	Secondary; Day
Enrolment	395 girls
Denomination	Roman Catholic
Fees	No

St Aengus Post-Primary

Address	Limerick Road, Mountrath, Co. Laois
Telephone	0502-32107
Email	aengus@iol.ie
Principal	Thomas Ryan
School Type	Vocational; Day
Enrolment	104 boys; 27 girls
Denomination	Interdenominational
Fees	No

Coláiste Iosagáin

Address	Portarlington, Co. Laois
Telephone	0502-23407
Email	pres@iol.ie
Principal	Seamus Bennett
School Type	Secondary; Day
Enrolment	331 boys; 368 girls
Denomination	Roman Catholic
Fees	No

Patrician College

Address	Ballyfin, Portlaoise, Co. Laois
Telephone	0502-55245
Email	office@ballyfin.com
Principal	Br Matthew P Hayes
School Type	Secondary; Day
Enrolment	272 boys; 176 girls
Denomination	Roman Catholic
Fees	No

Portlaoise College

Address	Mountrath Road, Portlaoise, Co. Laois
Telephone	057-8621480
Email	portvs@eircom.net
Principal	Michael Parsons
School Type	Vocational; Day
Enrolment	62 boys; 206 girls
Denomination	Interdenominational
Fees	No

Scoil Chríost Rí Presentation College

Address	Portlaoise, Co. Laois
Telephone	0502-21441
Email	scrport@eircom.net
Principal	Helen O'Donnell
School Type	Secondary; Day
Enrolment	380 girls
Denomination	Roman Catholic
Fees	No

St Mary's CBS

Address	Tower Hill, Portlaoise, Co. Laois
Telephone	0502-22849
Email	stmarycbs@eircom.net
Principal	Oliver Maher
School Type	Secondary; Day
Enrolment	393 boys
Denomination	Roman Catholic
Fees	No

St Fergal's College

Address	Rathdowney, Co. Laois
Telephone	0505-46357
Email	stfergalscollege@eircom.ie
Principal	Aine O'Neill
School Type	Vocational; Day
Enrolment	170 boys; 144 girls
Denomination	Interdenominational
Fees	No

Ballinamore Post-Primary Schools

Address	Ballinamore, Co. Leitrim
Telephone	071-9644049
Email	felims.ias@eircom.net
Principal	Fr Francis Duffy, Brendan Burns
School Type	Vocational / Secondary; Day
Enrolment	131 boys; 158 girls
Denomination	Interdenominational
Fees	No

Carrick-on-Shannon Community School

Address	Carrick-on-Shannon, Co. Leitrim
Telephone	071-9620880
Email	jflynn@carrickcs.ie
Principal	Joseph Flynn
School Type	Community; Day
Enrolment	338 boys; 331 girls
Denomination	Interdenominational
Fees	No

Carrigallen Vocational School

Address	Carrigallen, Co. Leitrim
Telephone	049-4339640
Email	vscallen@eircom.net
Principal	Eamonn Daly
School Type	Vocational; Day
Enrolment	123 boys; 102 girls
Denomination	Interdenominational
Fees	No

CO. LEITRIM

Lough Allen College

Address	Drumkeerin, Co. Leitrim
Telephone	071-9648017
Email	lac.ias@eircom.net
Principal	Stephanie Gibbons
School Type	Vocational; Day
Enrolment	113 boys; 122 girls
Denomination	Interdenominational
Fees	No

Vocational School

Address	Drumshambo, Co. Leitrim
Telephone	071-9641085
Email	info@dvs.ie
Principal	Emmanuel McCormack
School Type	Vocational; Day
Enrolment	164 boys; 156 girls
Denomination	Interdenominational
Fees	No

St Clare's Comprehensive School

Address	Manorhamilton, Co. Leitrim
Telephone	071-9855087
Email	stclares@iol.ie
Principal	John Irwin
School Type	Comprehensive; Day
Enrolment	182 boys; 234 girls
Denomination	Interdenominational
Fees	No

Marian College

Address	Mohill, Co. Leitrim
Telephone	071-9631208
Email	mcss@eircom.net
Principal	Una Duffy
School Type	Secondary; Day
Enrolment	85 boys; 143 girls
Denomination	Roman Catholic
Fees	No

Mohill Vocational School

Address	Mohill, Co. Leitrim
Telephone	071-9631122
Email	mohillvocationalschool@eircom.net
Principal	Martin Fallon
School Type	Vocational; Day
Enrolment	86 boys; 39 girls
Denomination	Interdenominational
Fees	No

Ardscoil Mhuire

Address	Corbally, Limerick
Telephone	061-349014
Email	mcla.ias@eircom.net
Principal	Colette McGrath
School Type	Secondary; Day
Enrolment	291 girls
Denomination	Roman Catholic
Fees	No

St Munchin's College

Address	Corbally, Limerick
Telephone	061-348922
Email	stmunchin@eircom.net
Principal	Rev Leslie McNamara
School Type	Secondary; Day
Enrolment	541 boys
Denomination	Roman Catholic
Fees	No

Ardscoil Rís

Address	North Circular Road, Limerick
Telephone	061-453828
Email	asroffice@eircom.net
Principal	Bríd de Brún
School Type	Secondary; Day
Enrolment	708 boys
Denomination	Roman Catholic
Fees	No

LIMERICK

Coláiste Mhichil

Address	Sexton Street, Limerick
Telephone	061-416628
Email	rice@iol.ie
Principal	N. Earlie
School Type	Secondary; Day
Enrolment	536 boys
Denomination	Roman Catholic
Fees	No

Crescent College Comprehensive SJ

Address	Dooradoyle Road, Dooradoyle, Limerick
Telephone	061-229655
Email	cccadmin.ias@eircom.net
Principal	Dermot Cowhey
School Type	Comprehensive; Day
Enrolment	523 boys; 356 girls
Denomination	Roman Catholic
Fees	No

Edmund Rice College

Address	Shelbourne Road, Limerick
Telephone	061-452079
Email	mariagoodwin@hotmail.com
Principal	Brian Finn
School Type	Secondary; Day
Enrolment	22 boys
Denomination	Roman Catholic
Fees	No

Laurel Hill Coláiste FCJ

Address	Cnoc na Labhras, Luimneach
Telephone	061-313636
Email	principal@laurelhillcolaistefcj.ie
Principal	Anne Mordan
School Type	Secondary; Day; All tuition through Irish
Enrolment	371 girls
Denomination	Roman Catholic
Fees	No

Laurel Hill Secondary School FCJ

Address	Laurel Hill, South Circular Road, Limerick
Telephone	061-319383
Email	principal@laurelhillfcj.ie
Principal	Adrian Cantillon
School Type	Secondary; Day
Enrolment	577 girls
Denomination	Roman Catholic
Fees	No

Limerick Senior College

Address	Mulgrave Street, Limerick
Telephone	061-414344
Email	mfitzgerald@limericksc.ie
Principal	Michael Fitzgerald
School Type	Vocational; Day
Enrolment	102 boys; 563 girls
Denomination	Interdenominational
Fees	No

Presentation Secondary School

Address	Sexton Street, Limerick
Telephone	061-410390
Email	psspupil@eircom.net
Principal	Michael Culhane
School Type	Secondary; Day
Enrolment	24 boys; 501 girls
Denomination	Roman Catholic
Fees	No

St Clement's College

Address	South Circular Road, Limerick
Telephone	061-315878
Email	clements_limk@eircom.net
Principal	Vincent Foley
School Type	Secondary; Day
Enrolment	404 boys
Denomination	Roman Catholic
Fees	No

St Enda's Community School

Address	Kilmallock Road, Limerick
Telephone	061-419222
Email	stendas1@iol.ie
Principal	Pat O'Brien
School Type	Community; Day
Enrolment	165 boys; 104 girls
Denomination	Interdenominational
Fees	No

St Nessan's Community College

Address	Moylish Park, Moylish, Limerick
Telephone	061-452422
Email	stnesscc.ias@eircom.net
Principal	Eugene O'Brien
School Type	Vocational; Day
Enrolment	273 boys; 239 girls
Denomination	Interdenominational
Fees	No

Salesian Secondary School

Address	Fernbank, North Circular Road, Limerick
Telephone	061-454093
Email	info@salesiansecondaryschool.ie
Principal	Brigid O'Connell
School Type	Secondary; Day
Enrolment	422 girls
Denomination	Roman Catholic
Fees	No

Scoil Carmel

Address	O'Connell Avenue, Limerick
Telephone	061-229511
Email	scoilcarmellim.ias@eircom.net
Principal	Elizabeth Flanagan
School Type	Secondary; Day
Enrolment	520 girls
Denomination	Roman Catholic
Fees	No

Villiers Seconday School

Address	North Circular Road, Limerick
Telephone	061-451447
Email	villiers@iol.ie
Principal	Thomas S Hardy
School Type	Secondary; Day & Boarding;
Enrolment	234 boys; 289 girls
Denomination	Church of Ireland
Fees	Day Yes Boarding Yes

St Ita's College

Address	Abbeyfeale, Co. Limerick
Telephone	068-31149
Email	itascol@eircom.net
Principal	Sean O Nialagain
School Type	Secondary; Day
Enrolment	133 boys
Denomination	Roman Catholic
Fees	No

St Joseph's Secondary School

Address	Convent of Mercy, Abbeyfeale, Co. Limerick
Telephone	068-31230
Email	conventschool.ias@tinet.ie
Principal	Edward O'Callaghan
School Type	Secondary; Day
Enrolment	360 girls
Denomination	Roman Catholic
Fees	No

Vocational School

Address	Abbeyfeale, Co. Limerick
Telephone	068-31198
Email	abbeyfeale@eircom.net
Principal	Tommy Barrett
School Type	Vocational; Day
Enrolment	253 boys; 68 girls
Denomination	Interdenominational
Fees	No

CO. LIMERICK

Coláiste Mhuire

Address	Askeaton, Co. Limerick
Telephone	061-392368
Email	colaistemhuire.ias@eircom.net
Principal	Mary Garvey
School Type	Vocational; Day
Enrolment	251 boys; 213 girls
Denomination	Interdenominational
Fees	No

Ard Scoil Mhuire FCJ

Address	Bruff, Kilmallock, Co. Limerick
Telephone	061-382349
Email	admin@fcjbruff.org
Principal	Michael Clifford
School Type	Seconday; Day & Boarding
Enrolment	125 boys; 140 girls
Denomination	Roman Catholic
Fees	Day No Boarding Yes

Coláiste Pobail Mhichíl

Address	Cappamore, Co. Limerick
Telephone	061-381272
Email	cappamorecc.ias@eircom.net
Principal	Mary Lysaght
School Type	Vocational; Day
Enrolment	54 boys; 60 girls
Denomination	Interdenominational
Fees	No

Coláiste Chiaráin

Address	Croom, Co. Limerick
Telephone	061-397700
Email	principal@cco.ie
Principal	Noel P Malone
School Type	Vocational; Day
Enrolment	216 boys; 245 girls
Denomination	Interdenominational
Fees	No

St Fintan's CBS

Address	Doon, Co. Limerick
Telephone	061-380388
Email	stfintansdoon@eircom.net
Principal	Edmond Bourke
School Type	Secondary; Day
Enrolment	274 boys
Denomination	Roman Catholic
Fees	No

St Joseph's Secondary School

Address	Convent of Mercy, Doon, Co. Limerick
Telephone	061-380378
Email	stjosephsdoonlimerick@eircom.net
Principal	Tom O'Dwyer
School Type	Secondary; Day
Enrolment	350 girls
Denomination	Roman Catholic
Fees	No

Hazelwood College

Address	Dromcollogher, Co. Limerick
Telephone	063-83121
Email	hazelc@hazelc.ie
Principal	Liam Lenihan
School Type	Vocational; Day
Enrolment	227 boys; 177 girls
Denomination	Interdenominational
Fees	No

John the Baptist Community School

Address	Hospital, Co. Limerick
Telephone	061-383283
Email	johnthebaptist.ias@eircom.net
Principal	James Twohig
School Type	Community; Day
Enrolment	317 boys; 338 girls
Denomination	Interdenominational
Fees	No

Scoil Pól

Address	Kilfinane, Co. Limerick
Telephone	063-91197
Email	secretary@scoilpol.ie
Principal	Sr Kathleen Neenan
School Type	Secondary; Day & Boarding
Enrolment	117 boys; 116 girls
Denomination	Roman Catholic
Fees	Day No Boarding Yes

Coláiste Iósaef

Address	Kilmallock, Co. Limerick
Telephone	063-98275
Email	admin@coliosaef.ie
Principal	Patrick J. McNamara
School Type	Vocational; Day
Enrolment	144 boys; 120 girls
Denomination	Interdenominational
Fees	No

Glenstal Abbey

Address	Murroe, Co. Limerick
Telephone	061-386099
Email	denis@glenstal.org
Principal	Br Denis Hooper, OSB
School Type	Secondary; Boarding only
Enrolment	198 boys
Denomination	Roman Catholic
Fees	Yes

Desmond College

Address	Gortboy, Newcastle West, Co. Limerick
Telephone	069-62205
Email	info@desmondcollege.ie
Principal	Pádraig Flanagan
School Type	Vocational; Day; One stream has all tuition through Irish
Enrolment	213 boys; 179 girls
Denomination	Interdenominational
Fees	No

Scoil Mhuire agus Íde

Address	Newcastle West, Co. Limerick
Telephone	069-62443
Email	smi@scoilmhuireaguside.com
Principal	S. O'Mahony-Kennedy
School Type	Secondary; Day
Enrolment	199 boys; 274 girls
Denomination	Roman Catholic
Fees	No

Castletroy College

Address	Newtown, Castletroy, Co. Limerick
Telephone	061-330785
Email	admin@castletroycollege.ie
Principal	Martin Wallace
School Type	Vocational; Day
Enrolment	476 boys; 449 girls
Denomination	Interdenominational
Fees	No

Salesian Secondary College

Address	Pallaskenry, Co. Limerick
Telephone	061-393105
Email	salesiansec@eircom.net
Principal	Paddy O'Neill
School Type	Secondary; Day
Enrolment	207 boys; 163 girls
Denomination	Roman Catholic
Fees	No

Coláiste na Trocaire

Address	Rathkeale, Co. Limerick
Telephone	069-64094
Email	mercycc@eircom.net
Principal	John Brouder
School Type	Vocational; Day
Enrolment	214 boys; 196 girls
Denomination	Interdenominational
Fees	No

Ballymahon Vocational School

Address	Ballymahon, Co. Longford
Telephone	090-6432211
Email	balvoc@unison.ie
Principal	John O'Donnell
School Type	Vocational; Day
Enrolment	125 boys; 74 girls
Denomination	Interdenominational
Fees	No

Mercy Secondary School

Address	Ballymahon, Co. Longford
Telephone	090-6432267
Email	mssballymahon@eircom.net
Principal	Jimmy Lennon
School Type	Secondary; Day
Enrolment	164 boys; 228 girls
Denomination	Roman Catholic
Fees	No

Ardscoil Phádraig

Address	Granard, Co. Longford
Telephone	043-86209
Email	apgran@iol.ie
Principal	R. Killian-Johnston
School Type	Vocational; Day
Enrolment	71 boys; 47 girls
Denomination	Interdenominational
Fees	No

Cnoc Mhuire

Address	Convent of Mercy, Granard, Co. Longford
Telephone	043-86231
Email	cmss.ias@eircom.net
Principal	Michael Duffy
School Type	Secondary; Day
Enrolment	167 boys; 253 girls
Denomination	Roman Catholic
Fees	No

Lanesboro Community College

Address	Lanesboro, Co. Longford
Telephone	043-21139
Email	lanesborocc.ias@eircom.net
Principal	Jimmy Flanagan
School Type	Vocational; Day
Enrolment	100 boys; 89 girls
Denomination	Interdenominational
Fees	No

Meánscoil Muire

Address	Convent Road, Longford Town, Co. Longford
Telephone	043-46608
Email	scoilmlongford.ias@eircom.net
Principal	Mary Kenny
School Type	Secondary; Day
Enrolment	516 girls
Denomination	Roman Catholic
Fees	No

St Mel's College

Address	Longford Town, Co. Longford
Telephone	043-46469
Email	stmels@stmelscollege.ie
Principal	Denis Glennon
School Type	Secondary; Day
Enrolment	593 boys
Denomination	Roman Catholic
Fees	No

Moyne Community School

Address	Moyne, Co. Longford
Telephone	049-4335114
Email	moynecs@eircom.net
Principal	Liam Flanagan
School Type	Community; Day
Enrolment	325 boys; 312 girls
Denomination	Interdenominational
Fees	No

Templemichael College

Address	Templemichael, Longford
Telephone	043-45455
Email	templemc@eircom.net
Principal	Ann Heffron
School Type	Vocational; Day
Enrolment	106 boys; 159 girls
Denomination	Interdenominational
Fees	No

Ardee Community School

Address	Ardee, Co. Louth
Telephone	041-6853557
Email	ardeecommunityschool1@eircom.net
Principal	John Crilly
School Type	Community; Day
Enrolment	293 boys; 287 girls
Denomination	Interdenominational
Fees	No

Drogheda Grammar School

Address	Mornington Road, Drogheda, Co. Louth
Telephone	041-9838281
Email	droghedags.ias@eircom.net
Principal	Richard W. Schmidt
School Type	Secondary; Day & Boarding
Enrolment	122 boys; 98 girls
Denomination	Church of Ireland
Fees	Day Yes Boarding Yes

Our Lady's College

Address	Greenhills, Drogheda, Co. Louth
Telephone	041-9831219
Email	office@ourladys.ie
Principal	Pádraig Ó Broin
School Type	Secondary; Day
Enrolment	871 girls
Denomination	Roman Catholic
Fees	No

Sacred Heart School

Address	Sunnyside, Drogheda, Co. Louth
Telephone	041-9837812
Email	shschool@iol.ie
Principal	Mary Caffrey
School Type	Secondary; Day
Enrolment	548 girls
Denomination	Roman Catholic
Fees	No

St Joseph's CBS

Address	Newfoundwell Road, Drogheda, Co. Louth
Telephone	041-9837232
Email	cbsoffice@eircom.net
Principal	P. A. Nolan
School Type	Secondary; Day
Enrolment	628 boys
Denomination	Roman Catholic
Fees	No

St Mary's Diocesan School

Address	Beamore Road, Drogheda, Co. Louth
Telephone	041-9837581
Email	stmarysds.ias@eircom.net
Principal	Caroline Clarke
School Type	Secondary; Day
Enrolment	710 boys
Denomination	Roman Catholic
Fees	No

St Oliver's Community College

Address	Rathmullen, Drogheda, Co. Louth
Telephone	041-9838390
Email	info@socc.ie
Principal	Terry Mahon
School Type	Vocational; Day
Enrolment	564 boys; 477 girls
Denomination	Interdenominational
Fees	No

Bush Post Primary School

Address	Riverstown, Dundalk, Co. Louth
Telephone	042-9376246
Email	bush.ias@eircom.net
Principal	Martin O'Brien
School Type	Vocational; Day
Enrolment	245 boys; 198 girls
Denomination	Interdenominational
Fees	No

Dundalk Grammar School

Address	Dundalk, Co. Louth	
Telephone	042-9334459	
Email	info@dundalkgrammarschool.ie	
Principal	Cyril Drury	
School Type	Secondary; Day & Boarding	
Enrolment	279 boys; 206 girls	
Denomination	Church of Ireland	
Fees	Day Yes	Boarding Yes

De La Salle Secondary School

Address	Castleblayney Road, Dundalk, Co. Louth
Telephone	042-9331179
Email	baptist@iol.ie
Principal	Martin Brennan
School Type	Secondary; Day
Enrolment	583 boys
Denomination	Roman Catholic
Fees	No

O Fiaich College

Address	Dublin Road, Dundalk, Co. Louth
Telephone	042-9331398
Email	info@ofiaichcollege.ie
Principal	Pádraig McGovern
School Type	Vocational; Day
Enrolment	360 boys; 336 girls
Denomination	Interdenominational
Fees	No

St Louis Secondary School

Address	Dun Lughaidh, Dundalk, Co. Louth
Telephone	042-9334474
Email	info@stlouisdundalk.ie
Principal	John Weir
School Type	Secondary; Day
Enrolment	677 girls
Denomination	Roman Catholic
Fees	No

St Mary's College

Address	Dundalk, Co. Louth
Telephone	042-9339977
Email	marist@iol.ie
Principal	Con McGinley
School Type	Secondary; Day
Enrolment	454 boys; 213 girls
Denomination	Roman Catholic
Fees	No

St Vincent's Secondary School

Address	Seatown Place, Dundalk, Co. Louth
Telephone	042-9332790
Email	office@stvincents-dundalk.ie
Principal	Anne McDonnell
School Type	Secondary; Day
Enrolment	708 girls
Denomination	Roman Catholic
Fees	No

Coláiste Rís

Address	Chapel Street, Dundalk, Co. Louth
Telephone	042-9334336
Email	colris@eircom.net
Principal	Kevin Wynne
School Type	Secondary; Day; 1 stream has all tuition through Irish
Enrolment	388 boys; 118 girls
Denomination	Roman Catholic
Fees	No

Scoil Uí Mhuiri

Address	Skibblemore, Dunleer, Co. Louth
Telephone	041-6851344
Email	scoilui@eircom.net
Principal	Brid Rocks
School Type	Vocational; Day
Enrolment	213 boys; 144 girls
Denomination	Interdenominational
Fees	No

Scoil Damhnait

Address	Gob a'Choire, Acaill, Co. Mhuigheo
Telephone	098-45467
Email	principal@scoildamhnait.org
Principal	Maire Sweeney
School Type	Secondary; Day
Enrolment	66 boys; 55 girls
Denomination	Roman Catholic
Fees	No

McHale College

Address	Achill, Westport, Co. Mayo
Telephone	098-45139
Email	mchalecollege@eircom.net
Principal	Niall S. Ó Loinsigh
School Type	Vocational; Day
Enrolment	87 boys; 65 girls
Denomination	Interdenominational
Fees	No

Balla Secondary School

Address	Balla, Castlebar, Co. Mayo
Telephone	094-9365082
Email	balsec@eircom.net
Principal	Pat F. Sheridan
School Type	Secondary; Day
Enrolment	219 boys; 248 girls
Denomination	Roman Catholic
Fees	No

CO. MAYO

Moyne College

Address	Ballina, Co. Mayo
Telephone	096-21472
Email	moynecol@eircom.net
Principal	Terry McCole
School Type	Vocational; Day
Enrolment	133 boys; 126 girls
Denomination	Interdenominational
Fees	No

St Mary's Secondary School

Address	Convent of Mercy, Ballina, Co. Mayo
Telephone	096-70333
Email	smboffice@eircom.net
Principal	Patricia Sweeney
School Type	Secondary; Day
Enrolment	582 girls
Denomination	Roman Catholic
Fees	No

St Muredach's College

Address	Sligo Road, Ballina, Co. May
Telephone	096-21298
Email	stmuredach@eircom.net
Principal	Fr Martin Barrett
School Type	Secondary; Day
Enrolment	450 boys
Denomination	Roman Catholic
Fees	No

Ballinrobe Community School

Address	Convent Road, Ballinrobe, Co. Mayo
Telephone	094-9541777
Email	blrobesch@eircom.net
Principal	Luke O'Malley
School Type	Community; Day
Enrolment	229 boys; 231 girls
Denomination	Interdenominational
Fees	No

Ballyhaunis Community School

Address	Knock Road, Ballyhaunis, Co. Mayo
Telephone	094-9630235
Email	principalballyhauniscs@eircom.net
Principal	Pat McHugh
School Type	Community; Day
Enrolment	314 boys; 295 girls
Denomination	Interdenominational
Fees	No

Our Lady's Secondary School

Address	Belmullet, Co. Mayo
Telephone	097-81157
Email	ourladysbelmullet@eircom.net
Principal	Padraic Staunton
School Type	Secondary; Day
Enrolment	141 boys; 202 girls
Denomination	Roman Catholic
Fees	No

St Brendan's College

Address	Belmullet, Co. Mayo
Telephone	097-81437
Email	saintbrendans@eircom.net
Principal	Sabina Munnelly
School Type	Vocational; Day
Enrolment	203 boys; 226 girls
Denomination	Interdenominational
Fees	No

Davitt College

Address	Springfield, Castlebar, Co. Mayo
Telephone	094-9023060
Email	davitt.ias@eircom.net
Principal	Patrick Noone
School Type	Vocational; Day
Enrolment	247 boys; 351 girls
Denomination	Interdenominational
Fees	No

Naomh Iosaef Clochar na Trócaire

Address	Caislean an Bharraigh (Castlebar), Co. Mhaigh Eo
Telephone	094-9021406
Email	joseph.ias@eircom.net
Principal	Aine Uí Mhorain
School Type	Secondary; Day
Enrolment	583 girls
Denomination	Roman Catholic
Fees	No

St Gerald's College

Address	Newport Road, Castlebar, Co. Mayo
Telephone	094-9021383
Email	info@stgeraldscollege.com
Principal	Bernard Keeley
School Type	Secondary; Day
Enrolment	605 boys
Denomination	Roman Catholic
Fees	No

St Joseph's Secondary School

Address	Charlestown, Claremorris, Co. Mayo
Telephone	094-9254211
Email	stjosephsch@eircom.net
Principal	Sr Breege Brennan
School Type	Secondary; Day
Enrolment	111 boys; 123 girls
Denomination	Roman Catholic
Fees	No

St Colman's College

Address	Claremorris, Co. Mayo
Telephone	094-9371442
Email	colmans.ias@eircom.net
Principal	Daniel McHugh
School Type	Secondary; Day
Enrolment	370 boys
Denomination	Roman Catholic
Fees	No

Mount St Michael Secondary School

Address	Convent Road, Claremorris, Co. Mayo
Telephone	094-9371474
Email	mtmichael@eircom.net
Principal	Fionnghuala King
School Type	Secondary; Day
Enrolment	433 girls
Denomination	Roman Catholic
Fees	No

Jesus & Mary Secondary School

Address	Gortnor Abbey, Crossmolina, Co. Mayo
Telephone	096-31597
Email	office@gortnorabbey.ie
Principal	Geraldine Ruane
School Type	Secondary; Day
Enrolment	219 boys; 288 girls
Denomination	Roman Catholic
Fees	No

St Tiernan's College

Address	Crossmolina, Ballina, Co. Mayo
Telephone	096-31236
Email	sttiernans@eircom.net
Principal	Oliver Bolton
School Type	Vocational; Day
Enrolment	136 boys; 72 girls
Denomination	Interdenominational
Fees	No

St Joseph's Secondary School

Address	Foxford, Co. Mayo
Telephone	094-9256145
Email	info@stjosephsfoxford.com
Principal	Brendan Forde
School Type	Secondary; Day
Enrolment	145 boys; 169 girls
Denomination	Roman Catholic
Fees	No

St Patrick's College

Address	Lacken Cross, Killala, Co. Mayo
Telephone	096-34177
Email	lackent.ias@eircom.net
Principal	Tony McGarry
School Type	Vocational; Day
Enrolment	131 boys; 155 girls
Denomination	Interdenominational
Fees	No

St Louis Community School

Address	Kiltimagh, Co. Mayo
Telephone	094-9381228
Email	stlouis@iol.ie
Principal	Michael McFadden
School Type	Community; Day
Enrolment	254 boys; 319 girls
Denomination	Interdenominational
Fees	No

Sancta Maria College

Address	Louisburgh, Co. Mayo
Telephone	098-66342
Email	sanctamc@iol.ie
Principal	Vincent O'Loughlin
School Type	Secondary; Day
Enrolment	176 boys; 192 girls
Denomination	Roman Catholic
Fees	No

Coláiste Chomain

Address	Rossport, Ballina, Co. Mayo
Telephone	097-88940
Email	colchom@eircom.net
Principal	Micháel Ó hEalaithe
School Type	Vocational; Day; All tuition through Irish
Enrolment	43 boys; 37 girls
Denomination	Interdenominational
Fees	No

Scoil Muire agus Pádraig

Address	Swinford, Co. Mayo
Telephone	094-9251481
Email	scmp@iol.ie
Principal	John Gallagher
School Type	Secondary; Day
Enrolment	247 boys; 260 girls
Denomination	Roman Catholic
Fees	No

Coláiste Mhuire

Address	Tuar Mhic Eadaigh, Co. Mhaigh Eo
Telephone	094-9544107
Email	colmuirtuar@eircom.net
Principal	Padraig Ó Dufaigh
School Type	Secondary; Day; All tuition through Irish
Enrolment	78 boys; 93 girls
Denomination	Roman Catholic
Fees	No

Carrowbeg College

Address	Westport, Co. Mayo
Telephone	098-25241
Email	carrowbegcollege@eircom.net
Principal	Mary O'Connor
School Type	Vocational; Day
Enrolment	50 boys; 38 girls
Denomination	Interdenominational
Fees	No

Rice College

Address	Westport, Co. Mayo
Telephone	098-25698
Email	mcarney@ricecollegewestport.ie
Principal	Frank McCarrick
School Type	Secondary; Day
Enrolment	432 boys
Denomination	Roman Catholic
Fees	No

Sacred Heart School

Address	Westport, Co. Mayo
Telephone	098-26268
Email	shswport@iol.ie
Principal	Mary Ryan
School Type	Secondary; Day
Enrolment	573 girls
Denomination	Roman Catholic
Fees	No

Ashbourne Community School

Address	Deerpark, Ashbourne, Co. Meath
Telephone	01-8353066
Email	admin@ashcom.ie
Principal	Aine O'Sullivan
School Type	Community; Day
Enrolment	466 boys; 432 girls
Denomination	Interdenominational
Fees	No

Athboy Community School

Address	Athboy, Co. Meath
Telephone	046-9487894
Email	athboycs@eircom.net
Principal	Anthony Leavy
School Type	Community; Day
Enrolment	240 boys; 186 girls
Denomination	Interdenominational
Fees	No

St Peter's College

Address	Dunboyne, Co. Meath
Telephone	01-8252552
Email	stpeterscc.ias@eircom.net
Principal	Eamon Gaffney
School Type	Vocational; Day
Enrolment	464 boys; 451 girls
Denomination	Interdenominational
Fees	No

CO. MEATH

Dunshaughlin Community College

Address	Dunshaughlin, Co. Meath
Telephone	01-8259137
Email	office@duncc.ie
Principal	Seamus Ryan
School Type	Vocational; Day
Enrolment	522 boys; 369 girls
Denomination	Interdenominational
Fees	No

St Fintina's Post-Primary School

Address	Longwood, Enfield, Co. Meath
Telephone	046-9555018
Email	stfintina@eircom.net
Principal	Thomas Stack
School Type	Vocational; Day
Enrolment	101 boys; 61 girls
Denomination	Interdenominational
Fees	No

Franciscan College

Address	Gormanstown, Co. Meath	
Telephone	01-8412203	
Email	adminsec@gormanstoncollege.ie	
Principal	Proinsias Ó Laoi	
School Type	Secondary; Day & Boarding	
Enrolment	542 boys; 54 girls	
Denomination	Roman Catholic	
Fees	Day Yes	Boarding Yes

Eureka Secondary School

Address	Kells, Co. Meath
Telephone	046-9240132
Email	eurekaschool@iol.ie
Principal	Sr Joan Dunne
School Type	Secondary; Day
Enrolment	6 boys; 713 girls
Denomination	Roman Catholic
Fees	No

St Ciaran's Community School

Address	Navan Road, Kells, Co. Meath
Telephone	046-9241551
Email	sccsstaff@eircom.net
Principal	Dermot Carney
School Type	Community; Day
Enrolment	477 boys; 38 girls
Denomination	Interdenominational
Fees	No

St Oliver Post Primary

Address	Oldcastle, Kells, Co. Meath
Telephone	049-8541180
Email	secretary@stoliver.com
Principal	Finbarr O'Connor
School Type	Vocational; Day
Enrolment	193 boys; 147 girls
Denomination	Interdenominational
Fees	No

Beaufort College

Address	Trim Road, Navan, Co. Meath
Telephone	046-9028915
Email	beaufortcollege@eircom.net
Principal	John Condon
School Type	Vocational; Day
Enrolment	235 boys; 107 girls
Denomination	Interdenominational
Fees	No

Loreto Secondary School

Address	St Michael's, Navan, Co. Meath
Telephone	046-9023830
Email	stmichaelsloreto@eircom.net
Principal	Sr Elaine Troy
School Type	Secondary; Day
Enrolment	751 girls
Denomination	Roman Catholic
Fees	No

St Joseph's Secondary School

Address	Mercy Convent, Navan, Co. Meath
Telephone	046-9021830
Email	mercysecnavan.ias@eircom.net
Principal	Vincent Donovan
School Type	Secondary; Day
Enrolment	532 girls
Denomination	Roman Catholic
Fees	No

St Patrick's Classical School

Address	Moatlands, Navan, Co. Meath
Telephone	046-9023772
Email	stpatscs@iol.ie
Principal	Brian Kennedy
School Type	Secondary; Day
Enrolment	829 boys
Denomination	Roman Catholic
Fees	No

O'Carolan College

Address	Nobber, Co. Meath
Telephone	046-9052177
Email	ocarolanadmin@eircom.net
Principal	Brian Goggins
School Type	Vocational; Day
Enrolment	143 boys; 92 girls
Denomination	Interdenominational
Fees	No

Coláiste Pobail Ráth Cairn

Address	Ráth Cairn, Athboy, Co. Meath
Telephone	046-9432722
Email	psrathcairn@eircom.net
Principal	Macdara Ó Duillearga
School Type	Vocational; Day; All tuition through Irish
Enrolment	74 boys; 52 girls
Denomination	Interdenominational
Fees	No

Ratoath Community College

Address	Fairyhouse Racecourse, Ratoath, Co. Meath
Telephone	01-8254102
Email	ratoath@duncc.ie
Principal	Máire Ní Bhróithe
School Type	Vocational; Day
Enrolment	100 boys; 80 girls
Denomination	Interdenominational
Fees	No

Boyne Community School

Address	Trim, Co. Meath
Telephone	046-9481654
Email	trimcs@eircom.net
Principal	Cora Dunne
School Type	Community; Day
Enrolment	405 boys; 71 girls
Denomination	Interdenominational
Fees	No

Scoil Mhuire

Address	Convent of Mercy, Trim, Co. Meath
Telephone	046-9431439
Email	scoilmhuiretrim.ias@eircom.net
Principal	Jeremiah S. Kearney
School Type	Secondary; Day
Enrolment	594 girls
Denomination	Roman Catholic
Fees	No

Ballybay Community College

Address	Ballybay, Co. Monaghan
Telephone	042-9741093
Email	ballybaycc@eircom.net
Principal	Paddy Kerr
School Type	Vocational; Day
Enrolment	97 boys; 102 girls
Denomination	Interdenominational
Fees	No

CO. MONAGHAN

Inver College

Address	Carrickmacross, Co. Monaghan
Telephone	042-9661282
Email	inbhear.ias@eircom.net
Principal	Breda Moroney-Ward
School Type	Vocational; Day
Enrolment	308 boys; 265 girls
Denomination	Interdenominational
Fees	No

Patrician High School

Address	Carrickmacross, Co. Monaghan
Telephone	042-9661525
Email	pjdphs@yahoo.ie
Principal	Joseph Duffy
School Type	Secondary; Day
Enrolment	382 boys
Denomination	Roman Catholic
Fees	No

St Louis Secondary School

Address	Carrickmacross, Co. Monaghan
Telephone	042-9661587
Email	stlouiscmx@eircom.net
Principal	Art Agnew
School Type	Secondary; Day
Enrolment	568 girls
Denomination	Roman Catholic
Fees	No

Castleblayney College

Address	Dublin Road, Castleblayney, Co. Monaghan
Telephone	042-9740066
Email	info@cblayneycollege.com
Principal	Gerard Hand
School Type	Vocational; Day
Enrolment	163 boys; 157 girls
Denomination	Interdenominational
Fees	No

Our Lady's Secondary School

Address	Clastleblayney, Co. Monaghan
Telephone	042-9740351
Email	secretary@ourladys-blayney.ie
Principal	Gerard McGuill
School Type	Secondary; Day
Enrolment	256 boys; 339 girls
Denomination	Roman Catholic
Fees	No

Largy College

Address	Analore Road, Clones, Co. Monaghan
Telephone	047-51132
Email	admin@largy.ie
Principal	Jim O'Connor
School Type	Vocational; Day
Enrolment	228 boys; 231 girls
Denomination	Interdenominational
Fees	No

Beech Hill College

Address	Monaghan, Co. Monaghan
Telephone	047-81200
Email	jhbhc@eircom.net
Principal	John Heaphey
School Type	Vocational; Day
Enrolment	265 boys; 364 girls
Denomination	Interdenominational
Fees	No

Coláiste Oiriall

Address	Ard Féa, Muineachan (Monaghan), Co. Mhuineachain
Telephone	047-72344
Email	colaisteoiriall@eircom.net
Principal	Brendan O'Duffy
School Type	Vocational; All tuition through Irish
Enrolment	13 boys; 15 girls
Denomination	Interdenominational
Fees	No

Monaghan Collegiate School

Address	Corlatt, Monaghan, Co. Monaghan
Telephone	047-82060
Email	mcs.ias@tinet.ie
Principal	Michael Hall
School Type	Secondary; Day
Enrolment	100 boys; 103 girls
Denomination	Church of Ireland
Fees	Yes

St Louis Secondary School

Address	Monaghan, Co. Monaghan
Telephone	047-81422
Email	stlouissecondaryschool@eircom.net
Principal	Vera O'Brien
School Type	Secondary; Day
Enrolment	793 girls
Denomination	Roman Catholic
Fees	No

St Macartan's College

Address	Monaghan, Co. Monaghan
Telephone	047-81642
Email	office@stmacs.com
Principal	Paraic Duffy
School Type	Secondary; Day
Enrolment	675 boys
Denomination	Roman Catholic
Fees	No

La Sainte Union Secondary School

Address	Banagher, Co. Offaly
Telephone	0509-51406
Email	lsuprincipal@eircom.net
Principal	Tom McGlacken
School Type	Secondary; Day
Enrolment	97 boys; 160 girls
Denomination	Roman Catholic
Fees	No

CO. OFFALY

Saint Rynagh's Community College

Address	Banagher, Co. Offaly
Telephone	0509-51323
Email	admin@strynaghs.org
Principal	Nora Kennedy
School Type	Vocational; Day
Enrolment	204 boys; 174 girls
Denomination	Interdenominational
Fees	No

St Brendan's Community School

Address	Birr, Co. Offaly
Telephone	0509-20510
Email	stbrnbir@iol.ie
Principal	Tom Foley
School Type	Community; Day
Enrolment	365 boys; 354 girls
Denomination	Interdenominational
Fees	No

Ard Scoil Chiaráin Naofa

Address	Frederick Street, Clara, Co. Offaly
Telephone	057 9331231
Email	claravs.ias@eircom.net
Principal	Dominic Guinan
School Type	Vocational; Day; At least one subject other than Irish taught through Irish
Enrolment	100 boys; 115 girls
Denomination	Interdenominational
Fees	No

Oaklands Community College

Address	Sr Senan Avenue, Edenderry, Co. Offaly
Telephone	046-9731573
Email	oakland.ias@eircom.net
Principal	Michael Dineen
School Type	Vocational; Day
Enrolment	221 boys; 127 girls
Denomination	Interdenominational
Fees	No

St Mary's Secondary School

Address	Edenderry, Co. Offaly
Telephone	046-9731457
Email	stmaryedy.ias@tinet.ie
Principal	Bernadette O'Neill
School Type	Secondary; Day
Enrolment	277 boys; 393 girls
Denomination	Roman Catholic
Fees	No

Gallen Community School

Address	Ferbane, Co. Offaly
Telephone	0906-454548
Email	galseca@eircom.net
Principal	John Irwin
School Type	Community; Day
Enrolment	153 boys; 180 girls
Denomination	Interdenominational
Fees	No

Coláiste Naomh Cormac

Address	Kilcormac, Co. Offaly
Telephone	0509-35048
Email	kilcorma@iol.ie
Principal	Tom Donoghue
School Type	Vocational; Day
Enrolment	148 boys; 125 girls
Denomination	Interdenominational
Fees	No

Killina Presentation Secondary School

Address	Rahan, Tullamore, Co. Offaly
Telephone	0506-55706
Email	killina.ias@eircom.net
Principal	Carthagena Minnock
School Type	Secondary; Day
Enrolment	255 boys; 212 girls
Denomination	Roman Catholic
Fees	No

Coláiste Choilm

Address	O'Moore Street, Tullamore, Co. Offaly
Telephone	0506-51756
Email	cbstullamore.ias@eircom.net
Principal	Colin Roddy
School Type	Secondary; Day
Enrolment	350 boys
Denomination	Roman Catholic
Fees	No

Sacred Heart School

Address	Tullamore, Co. Offaly
Telephone	0506-21747
Email	shs@eircom.ie
Principal	Sheila McManamly
School Type	Secondary; Day
Enrolment	670 girls
Denomination	Roman Catholic
Fees	No

Tullamore College

Address	Riverside, Tullamore, Co. Offaly
Telephone	0506-21677
Email	tullcoll@iol.ie
Principal	Edward McEvoy
School Type	Vocational; Day
Enrolment	333 boys; 154 girls
Denomination	Interdenominational
Fees	No

St Nathy's College

Address	Ballaghaderreen, Co. Roscommon
Telephone	094-9860010
Email	stnathys@iol.ie
Principal	Rev. Dr Martin Convey
School Type	Secondary; Day
Enrolment	302 boys; 304 girls
Denomination	Roman Catholic
Fees	No

CO. ROSCOMMON

Abbey Community College

Address	Boyle, Co. Roscommon
Telephone	071-9664646
Email	info@abbeycc.ie
Principal	Sean Tansey
School Type	Vocational; Day
Enrolment	188 boys; 256 girls
Denomination	Interdenominational
Fees	No

Castlerea Community School

Address	Castlerea, Co. Roscommon
Telephone	094-9620177
Email	marymull@eircom.net
Principal	Mary Mullarkey
School Type	Vocational; Day
Enrolment	270 boys; 277 girls
Denomination	Interdenominational
Fees	No

Elphin Community College

Address	Elphin, Castlerea, Co. Roscommon
Telephone	071-9635031
Email	elphincc@eircom.net
Principal	Elma Nerney
School Type	Vocational; Day
Enrolment	69 boys; 47 girls
Denomination	Interdenominational
Fees	No

CBS Roscommon

Address	Abbeytown, Roscommon, Co. Roscommon
Telephone	090-6626496
Email	cbsroscommon@eircom.net
Principal	Michael Fahey
School Type	Secondary; Day
Enrolment	316 boys
Denomination	Roman Catholic
Fees	No

Roscommon Community College

Address	Lisnamult, Roscommon, Co. Roscommon
Telephone	090-6626670
Email	roscolcom@eircom.net
Principal	Frank Chambers
School Type	Vocational; Day
Enrolment	79 boys; 26 girls
Denomination	Interdenominational
Fees	No

Scoil Mhuire gan Smál

Address	Convent of Mercy, Roscommon, Co. Roscommon
Telephone	090-6626321
Email	roscon@iol.ie
Principal	Tom Judge
School Type	Secondary; Day
Enrolment	519 girls
Denomination	Roman Catholic
gFees	No

Scoil Mhuire

Address	Strokestown, Co. Roscommon
Telephone	078-33223
Email	scoilmhuirestrokestown@eircom.net
Principal	Paul Costello
School Type	Secondary; Day
Enrolment	211 boys; 202 girls
Denomination	Roman Catholic
Fees	No

Ballinode College

Address	Ballinode, Sligo
Telephone	071-9145480
Email	ballinodecollege@eircom.net
Principal	Justin McCarthy
School Type	Vocational; Day
Enrolment	143 boys; 106 girls
Denomination	Interdenominational
Fees	No

CO. SLIGO

St Attracta's Community School

Address	Ballyara, Tubbercurry, Co. Sligo
Telephone	071-9120814
Email	stattractas@tubcc.ie
Principal	William Ruane
School Type	Community; Day
Enrolment	237 boys; 274 girls
Denomination	Interdenominational
Fees	No

Coláiste Mhuire

Address	Ballymote, Co. Sligo
Telephone	071-9183086
Email	ballymotecm.ias@eircom.net
Principal	Marie Johnson
School Type	Secondary; Day
Enrolment	170 boys; 193 girls
Denomination	Roman Catholic
Fees	No

Corran College

Address	Ballymote, Co. Sligo
Telephone	071-9183285
Email	corrancollege1@eircom.net
Principal	Colette O'Hagan
School Type	Vocational; Day
Enrolment	40 boys; 29 girls
Denomination	Interdenominational
Fees	No

St Mary's College

Address	Ballysadare, Co. Sligo
Telephone	071-9167579
Email	stmaryscollege.ias@eircom.net
Principal	Sr Mary Glynn
School Type	Secondary; Day
Enrolment	265 boys; 227 girls
Denomination	Roman Catholic
Fees	No

Coláiste Iascaigh

Address	Easkey, Co. Sligo
Telephone	096-49021
Email	colaisteiascaigh@eircom.net
Principal	Rosaleen Oldfield
School Type	Vocational; Day
Enrolment	44 boys; 49 girls
Denomination	Interdenominational
Fees	No

Jesus & Mary Secondary School

Address	Enniscrone, Co. Sligo
Telephone	096-36496
Email	jmsschool@eircom.net
Principal	Sr Mary Kelly
School Type	Secondary; Day
Enrolment	136 boys; 223 girls
Denomination	Roman Catholic
Fees	No

Grange Vocational School

Address	Grange, Co. Sligo
Telephone	071-9163514
Email	grangevs@iol.ie
Principal	Eamonn B. A. Tolan
School Type	Vocational; Day
Enrolment	66 boys; 21 girls
Denomination	Interdenominational
Fees	No

Gurteen Vocational School

Address	Gurteen, Ballymote, Co. Sligo
Telephone	071-9182383
Email	gurteenvec.ias@eircom.net
Principal	Christy Gallagher
School Type	Vocational; Day
Enrolment	21 boys; 20 girls
Denomination	Interdenominational
Fees	No

Coola Post-Primary School

Address	Riverstown, via Boyle, Co. Sligo
Telephone	071-9165365
Email	principal@coola.ie
Principal	Damien McGoldrick
School Type	Vocational; Day
Enrolment	153 boys; 107 girls
Denomination	Interdenominational
Fees	No

Mercy College

Address	Sligo Town, Co. Sligo
Telephone	071-9143476
Email	mercyso.ias@eircom.net
Principal	Sr Mary Forde
School Type	Secondary; Day
Enrolment	14 boys; 512 girls
Denomination	Roman Catholic
Fees	No

Sligo Grammar School

Address	The Mall, Sligo
Telephone	071-9145010
Email	admin@sligogrammarschool.iol.ie
Principal	Wynn A. Oliver
School Type	Secondary; Day & Boarding
Enrolment	253 boys; 183 girls
Denomination	Church of Ireland
Fees	Day Yes Boarding Yes

Ursuline College

Address	Finisklin, Sligo
Telephone	071-9161653
Email	ucsoffice@eircom.net
Principal	Sr Mairead O'Regan
School Type	Secondary; Day
Enrolment	650 girls
Denomination	Roman Catholic
Fees	No

Summerhill College

Address	Sligo Town, Co. Sligo
Telephone	071-9160311
Email	summerhill@esatclear.ie
Principal	Michael Murphy
School Type	Secondary; Day
Enrolment	712 boys
Denomination	Roman Catholic
Fees	No

North Connaught College

Address	Tubbercurry, Co. Sligo
Telephone	071-9185035
Email	ccn.ias@eircom.net
Principal	Mary Madden
School Type	Vocational; Day
Enrolment	14 boys; 51 girls
Denomination	Interdenominational
Fees	No

Presentation Secondary School

Address	Ballingarry, Thurles, Co. Tipperary
Telephone	052-54104
Email	presballingarry@eircom.net
Principal	Tom Fennessey
School Type	Secondary; Day
Enrolment	122 boys; 198 girls
Denomination	Roman Catholic
Fees	No

Borrisokane Community School

Address	Borrisokane, Co. Tipperary
Telephone	067-27268
Email	borris@iol.ie
Principal	Matthew Carr
School Type	Vocational; Day
Enrolment	244 boys; 217 girls
Denomination	Interdenominational
Fees	No

CO. TIPPERARY

St Joseph's College

Address	Borrisoleigh, Thurles, Co. Tipperary
Telephone	0504-51215
Email	stjosephsborris@hotmail.com
Principal	Padraig O'Shea
School Type	Secondary; Day
Enrolment	211 boys; 184 girls
Denomination	Roman Catholic
Fees	No

Coláiste Dun Iascaigh

Address	Cashel Road, Cahir, Co. Tipperary
Telephone	052-42828
Email	dunias.ias@eircom.net
Principal	Mary Finnegan-Burke
School Type	Vocational; Day
Enrolment	317 boys; 317 girls
Denomination	Interdenominational
Fees	No

CBS Secondary School

Address	Mount St Nicholas, Carrick-on-Suir, Co. Tipperary
Telephone	051-640522
Email	cbscos@eircom.net
Principal	Billy O'Farrell
School Type	Secondary; Day
Enrolment	190 boys
Denomination	Roman Catholic
Fees	No

Scoil Mhuire

Address	Greenhill, Carrick-on-Suir, Co. Tipperary
Telephone	051-640383
Email	greenhill@eircom.net
Principal	Mary O'Keeffe
School Type	Secondary; Day
Enrolment	400 girls
Denomination	Roman Catholic
Fees	No

Carrick-on-Suir Vocational School

Address	Carrick-on-Suir, Co. Tipperary
Telephone	051-640131
Email	cosvec@eircom.ie
Principal	Patrick Callanan
School Type	Vocational; Day
Enrolment	194 boys; 82 girls
Denomination	Interdenominational
Fees	No

Cashel Community School

Address	Dualla Road, Cashel, Co. Tipperary
Telephone	062-61167
Email	cashelcs.ias@eircom.net
Principal	Eddie Morrissey
School Type	Community; Day
Enrolment	425 boys; 389 girls
Denomination	Interdenominational
Fees	No

Rockwell College

Address	Cashel, Co. Tipperary
Telephone	062-61444
Email	info@rockwell-college.ie
Principal	Pat O'Sullivan
School Type	Secondary; Day & Boarding
Enrolment	341 boys; 147 girls
Denomination	Roman Catholic
Fees	Day No Boarding Yes

Ardscoil na mBráithre

Address	Clonmel, Co. Tipperary
Telephone	052-24459
Email	info@cbshighschoolclonmel.ie
Principal	Seamus Bannon
School Type	Secondary; Day
Enrolment	703 boys
Denomination	Roman Catholic
Fees	No

Central Technical Institute

Address	Clonmel, Co. Tipperary
Telephone	052-21450
Email	info@cti-clonmel.ie
Principal	Charlie McGeever
School Type	Vocational; Day
Enrolment	178 boys; 155 girls
Denomination	Interdenominational
Fees	No

Loreto Secondary School

Address	Coleville Road, Clonmel, Co. Tipperary
Telephone	052-21402
Email	loretoclonmel@eircom.net
Principal	Sr Bridie Mullins
School Type	Secondary; Day
Enrolment	495 girls
Denomination	Roman Catholic
Fees	No

Presentation Secondary School

Address	Clonmel, Co. Tipperary
Telephone	052-23587
Email	presedsec@eircom.net
Principal	Anne Breen
School Type	Secondary; Day
Enrolment	475 girls
Denomination	Roman Catholic
Fees	No

Patrician Presentation Secondary School

Address	Rocklow Road, Fethard, Co. Tipperary
Telephone	052-31572
Email	ppssadmin@gmail.com
Principal	Ernan Britton
School Type	Secondary; Day
Enrolment	93 boys; 63 girls
Denomination	Roman Catholic
Fees	No

Scoil Ruain

Address	Killenaule, Thurles, Co. Tipperary
Telephone	052-56332
Email	scoilruain.ias@tinet.ie
Principal	Colette Treacy
School Type	Vocational; Day
Enrolment	237 boys; 164 girls
Denomination	Interdenominational
Fees	No

Nenagh Vocational School

Address	Dromin Road, Nenagh, Co. Tipperary
Telephone	067-31525
Email	nenavoc@eircom.net
Principal	Michael McNulty
School Type	Vocational; Day; At least one subject other than Irish taught through Irish
Enrolment	138 boys; 236 girls
Denomination	Interdenominational
Fees	No

St Joseph's CBS

Address	Summerhill, Nenagh, Co. Tipperary
Telephone	067-34789
Email	cbsnen.ias@eircom.net
Principal	Raymond E Cowan
School Type	Secondary; Day
Enrolment	428 boys
Denomination	Roman Catholic
Fees	No

St Mary's Secondary School

Address	Nenagh, Co. Tipperary
Telephone	067-31450
Email	stmarysnenagh.ias@eircom.net
Principal	Jeremiah Cronin
School Type	Secondary; Day
Enrolment	536 girls
Denomination	Roman Catholic
Fees	No

St Joseph's College

Address	Black Road, Newport, Co. Tipperary
Telephone	061-378262
Email	newportcollege@eircom.net
Principal	Linda Kiely
School Type	Vocational; Day
Enrolment	102 boys; 69 girls
Denomination	Interdenominational
Fees	No

St Mary's Secondary School

Address	Newport, Co. Tipperary
Telephone	061-378344
Email	-------
Principal	Patrick O'Toole
School Type	Secondary; Day
Enrolment	183 boys; 202 girls
Denomination	Roman Catholic
Fees	No

Cistercian College

Address	Roscrea, Co. Tipperary
Telephone	0505-23344
Email	mtjoseph@iol.ie
Principal	Hugh McDonnell
School Type	Secondary; Boarding only
Enrolment	269 boys
Denomination	Roman Catholic
Fees	Yes

Coláiste Phobail Ros Cré

Address	Corville Road, Roscrea, Co. Tipperary
Telephone	0505-23939
Email	roscrea@cpr.ie
Principal	Gerard O'Brien
School Type	Vocational; Day
Enrolment	332 boys; 358 girls
Denomination	Interdenominational
Fees	No

Our Lady's Secondary School

Address	Templemore, Co. Tipperary
Telephone	0504-31299
Email	office@ourladystemplemore.ie
Principal	Patricia Higgins
School Type	Secondary; Day
Enrolment	293 boys; 219 girls
Denomination	Roman Catholic
Fees	No

St Sheelan's College

Address	Templemore, Co. Tipperary
Telephone	0504-31007
Email	sheelan@iol.ie
Principal	Daniel Condren
School Type	Vocational; Day
Enrolment	25 boys; 147 girls
Denomination	Interdenominational
Fees	No

CBS Thurles

Address	O'Donovan Rossa Street, Thurles, Co. Tipperary
Telephone	0504-22054
Email	reception@cbsthurles.ie
Principal	Martin Quirke
School Type	Secondary; Day
Enrolment	448 boys
Denomination	Roman Catholic
Fees	No

Presentation Secondary School

Address	Thurles, Co. Tipperary	
Telephone	0504-22291	
Email	pressec.ias@tinet.ie	
Principal	Jean Butler	
School Type	Secondary; Day & Boarding	
Enrolment	443 girls	
Denomination	Roman Catholic	
Fees	Day No	Boarding Yes

Ursuline Secondary School

Address	Thurles, Co. Tipperary
Telephone	0504-22147
Email	sec.uct@oceanfree.net
Principal	Sr Whelan
School Type	Secondary; Day & Boarding
Enrolment	702 girls
Denomination	Roman Catholic
Fees	Day No Boarding Yes

Gairm Scoil Mhuire

Address	Castlemeadows, Thurles, Co. Tipperary
Telephone	0504-21734
Email	gairmscoilmt.ias@tinet.ie
Principal	Fiona O'Sullivan
School Type	Vocational; Day; One stream has all tuition through Irish
Enrolment	166 boys; 192 girls
Denomination	Interdenominational
Fees	No

St Ailbe's School

Address	Rosanna Road, Tipperary Town
Telephone	062-51905
Email	scoil@ailbes.com
Principal	Paul O'Callaghan
School Type	Vocational; Day
Enrolment	142 boys; 196 girls
Denomination	Interdenominational
Fees	No

St Anne's Secondary School

Address	Convent of Mercy, Rosanna Road, Tipperary Town
Telephone	062-51747
Email	stanness@iol.ie
Principal	Donald O'Bryne
School Type	Secondary; Day
Enrolment	335 girls
Denomination	Roman Catholic
Fees	No

The Abbey School

Address	Station Road, Tipperary Town, Co. Tipperary
Telephone	062-52299
Email	abbeyoffice@eircom.net
Principal	John Heffernan
School Type	Secondary; Day
Enrolment	439 boys
Denomination	Roman Catholic
Fees	No

Abbey Community College

Address	Ferrybank, Waterford
Telephone	051-832930
Email	admin@abbeycommunitycollege.com
Principal	Tommy Lannigan
School Type	Vocational; Day
Enrolment	215 boys; 310 girls
Denomination	Interdenominational
Fees	No

Central Technical Institute

Address	Parnell Street, Waterford City
Telephone	051-874053
Email	centechw@iol.ie
Principal	Gerard Morgan
School Type	Vocational; Day
Enrolment	133 boys; 560 girls
Denomination	Interdenominational
Fees	No

CBS Mount Sion

Address	Barrack Street, Waterford
Telephone	051-377378
Email	mtsion.ias@eircom.net
Principal	Robert McCarthy
School Type	Secondary; Day
Enrolment	237 boys
Denomination	Roman Catholic
Fees	No

CO. WATERFORD

De La Salle College

Address	Newtown, Waterford
Telephone	051-875294
Email	admin@delasallewaterford.ie
Principal	Br Damien Kellegher, FSC
School Type	Secondary; Day
Enrolment	945 boys; 43 girls
Denomination	Roman Catholic
Fees	No

Newtown School

Address	Waterford City	
Telephone	051-860200	
Email	hpcollins@newtownschool.ie	
Principal	H. P. Collins	
School Type	Secondary; Day & Boarding	
Enrolment	177 boys; 179 girls	
Denomination	Mormon	
Fees	Day Yes	Boarding Yes

Our Lady of Mercy Secondary School

Address	Ozanam Street, Waterford
Telephone	051-373476
Email	mersec@iol.ie
Principal	Michael Lane
School Type	Secondary; Day
Enrolment	700 girls
Denomination	Roman Catholic
Fees	No

Presentation Secondary School

Address	Cannon Street, Waterford City
Telephone	051-376584
Email	pressch@eircom.net
Principal	Terence White
School Type	Secondary; Day
Enrolment	447 girls
Denomination	Roman Catholic
Fees	No

St Angela's

Address	Ursuline Convent, Waterford
Telephone	051-876510
Email	office@ursulinewaterford.ie
Principal	Margaret O'Donovan
School Type	Secondary; Day
Enrolment	805 girls
Denomination	Roman Catholic
Fees	No

St Paul's Community College

Address	Browne's Road, Waterford City
Telephone	051-355816
Email	stpaulscol@eircom.net
Principal	Anthony Condron
School Type	Vocational; Day
Enrolment	359 boys; 127 girls
Denomination	Interdenominational
Fees	No

Waterpark College

Address	Park Road, Waterford
Telephone	051-874445
Email	waterparkcollege@eircom.net
Principal	Thomas A. Beecher
School Type	Secondary; Day
Enrolment	265 boys
Denomination	Roman Catholic
Fees	No

Ard Scoil na nDéise

Address	Convent Road, Dungarvan, Co. Waterford
Telephone	058-41464
Email	ardscoil@cablesurf.com
Principal	Angela Conway
School Type	Secondary; Day
Enrolment	410 girls
Denomination	Roman Catholic
Fees	No

Coláiste Chathail Naofa

Address	Youghal Road, Dungarvan, Co. Waterford
Telephone	058-41184
Email	ccn@cablesurf.com
Principal	Patrick Buckley
School Type	Vocational; Day
Enrolment	121 boys; 241 girls
Denomination	Interdenominational
Fees	No

St Augustine's College

Address	Abbeyside, Dungarvan, Co. Waterford
Telephone	058-41140
Email	principal@staugustine.ie
Principal	Joseph A. Moynihan
School Type	Secondary; Day
Enrolment	323 boys; 260 girls
Denomination	Roman Catholic
Fees	No

Scoil na mBráithre

Address	Dungarvan, Co. Waterford
Telephone	058-41185
Email	gpower@cablesurf.com
Principal	Ann Prendergast
School Type	Secondary; Day
Enrolment	286 boys; 30 girls
Denomination	Roman Catholic
Fees	No

St Declan's Community College

Address	Kilmacthomas, Co. Waterford
Telephone	051-294100
Email	stdeclansccoffice@eircom.net
Principal	Sean Aherne
School Type	Vocational; Day
Enrolment	344 boys; 363 girls
Denomination	Interdenominational
Fees	No

Blackwater Community School

Address	Lismore, Co. Waterford
Telephone	058-53620
Email	tinamoore10@hotmail.com
Principal	Denis Ring
School Type	Community; Day
Enrolment	229 boys; 280 girls
Denomination	Interdenominational
Fees	No

Meánscoil San Nioclás

Address	Rinn O gCuanach, Co. Phort Lairge
Telephone	058-46464
Email	priomh.ias@eircom.net
Principal	Áine Ó Ceallaigh
School Type	Vocational; Day; All tuition through Irish
Enrolment	53 boys; 35 girls
Denomination	Interdenominational
Fees	No

CBS Tramore

Address	Tramore, Co. Waterford
Telephone	051-386766
Email	office@cbstramore.com
Principal	Gearóid M. O'Brien
School Type	Secondary; Day
Enrolment	400 boys
Denomination	Roman Catholic
Fees	No

Stella Maris

Address	Pond Road, Tramore, Co. Waterford
Telephone	051-381298
Email	smstafff.ias@tinet.ie
Principal	Sr M-T Porter
School Type	Secondary; Day
Enrolment	328 girls
Denomination	Roman Catholic
Fees	No

Athlone Community College

Address	Retreat Road, Athlone, Co. Westmeath
Telephone	0906-472640
Email	athlonecc@eircom.net
Principal	Val O'Connor
School Type	Vocational; Day; At least one subject other than Irish taught through Irish
Enrolment	577 boys; 311 girls
Denomination	Interdenominational
Fees	No

Marist College

Address	Retreat Road, Athlone, Co. Westmeath
Telephone	090-6474491
Email	tblaineprincpal@eircom.net
Principal	Thomas Blaine
School Type	Secondary; Day
Enrolment	378 boys
Denomination	Roman Catholic
Fees	No

Our Lady's Bower

Address	Retreat Road, Athlone, Co. Westmeath
Telephone	090-6474777
Email	bower@iol.ie
Principal	Sr Denise O'Brien
School Type	Secondary; Day & Boarding
Enrolment	609 girls
Denomination	Roman Catholic
Fees	Day No Boarding Yes

St Aloysius College

Address	The Park, Athlone, Co. Westmeath
Telephone	090-6492030
Email	staloysius.ias@eircom.net
Principal	Michael O Faolain
School Type	Secondary; Day
Enrolment	261 boys; 53 girls
Denomination	Roman Catholic
Fees	No

St Joseph's College

Address	Summerhill, Athlone, Co. Westmeath
Telephone	090-6492383
Email	stjossh@iol.ie
Principal	Mary Fahy
School Type	Secondary; Day
Enrolment	13 boys; 568 girls
Denomination	Roman Catholic
Fees	No

Castlepollard Community College

Address	Castlepollard, Mullingar, Co. Westmeath
Telephone	044-61163
Email	colaiste@eirom.net
Principal	James F. Whyte
School Type	Vocational; Day
Enrolment	69 boys; 83 girls
Denomination	Interdenominational
Fees	No

Meánscoil an Chlochair

Address	Kilbeggan, Mullingar, Co. Westmeath
Telephone	0506-32292
Email	kilcon.ias@tinet.ie
Principal	Catherine Moynihan
School Type	Secondary; Day
Enrolment	190 boys; 186 girls
Denomination	Roman Catholic
Fees	No

Columba College

Address	Killucan, Co. Westmeath
Telephone	044-74107
Email	columbacollege.ias@eircom.net
Principal	Maura McAuliffe
School Type	Vocational; Day
Enrolment	75 boys; 59 girls
Denomination	Interdenominational
Fees	No

Moate Community School

Address	Church Street, Moate, Co. Westmeath
Telephone	090-6481350
Email	mcsadmin@eircom.net
Principal	Kevin Duffy
School Type	Community; Day
Enrolment	367 boys; 619 girls
Denomination	Interdenominational
Fees	No

Coláiste Mhuire

Address	Mullingar, Co. Westmeath
Telephone	044-44743
Email	cbsadmin@eircom.net
Principal	John O'Meara
School Type	Secondary; Day
Enrolment	515 boys; 34 girls
Denomination	Roman Catholic
Fees	No

Loreto College

Address	Mullingar, Co. Westmeath
Telephone	044-42055
Email	loretomgar@eircom.ie
Principal	Michael G. Kearns
School Type	Secondary; Day
Enrolment	791 girls
Denomination	Roman Catholic
Fees	No

Mullingar Community College

Address	Millmount Road, Mullingar, Co. Westmeath
Telephone	044-40786
Email	mgarcc.ias@eircom.net
Principal	Ann Hanly
School Type	Vocational; Day
Enrolment	224 boys; 229 girls
Denomination	Interdenominational
Fees	No

St Finian's College

Address	Mullingar, Co. Westmeath
Telephone	044-48672
Email	paulconnell@eircom.ie
Principal	Fr Paul Connell
School Type	Secondary; Day & Boarding
Enrolment	337 boys; 96 girls
Denomination	Roman Catholic
Fees	Day No Boarding Yes

St Joseph's Secondary School

Address	Rochfortbridge, Mullingar, Co. Westmeath
Telephone	044-22176
Email	comrb@iol.ie
Principal	Anthony Hartnett
School Type	Secondary; Day
Enrolment	360 boys; 368 girls
Denomination	Roman Catholic
Fees	No

Wilson's Hospital School

Address	Multyfarnham, Co. Westmeath
Telephone	044-71115
Email	wilsonsh@iol.ie
Principal	Adrian G. Oughton
School Type	Secondary; Day & Boarding
Enrolment	191 boys; 210 girls
Denomination	Church of Ireland
Fees	Day Yes Boarding Yes

Coláiste Abbain

Address	Adamstown, Enniscorthy, Co. Wexford
Telephone	054-40564
Email	info@colaisteabbain.com
Principal	Senan Lillis
School Type	Vocational; Day
Enrolment	101 boys; 151 girls
Denomination	Interdenominational
Fees	No

CO. WEXFORD

Bridgetown Vocational College

Address	Bridgetown, Co. Wexford
Telephone	053-35257
Email	btownvc@iol.ie
Principal	Tony Power
School Type	Vocational; Day
Enrolment	348 boys; 246 girls
Denomination	Interdenominational
Fees	No

FCJ Secondary School

Address	Bunclody, Enniscorthy, Co. Wexford
Telephone	054-77308
Email	bunfcj@eircom.net
Principal	Sr Madeleine Ryan
School Type	Secondary; Day
Enrolment	329 boys; 380 girls
Denomination	Roman Catholic
Fees	No

Bunclody Vocational College

Address	Bunclody, Enniscorthy, Co. Wexford
Telephone	054-77590
Email	bunclodi.ias@eircom.net
Principal	William Corcoran
School Type	Vocational; Day
Enrolment	104 boys; 191 girls
Denomination	Interdenominational
Fees	No

Coláiste Bríde

Address	Enniscorthy, Co. Wexford
Telephone	054-34245
Email	colaistebride1@hotmail.com
Principal	Thomas Sheridan
School Type	Secondary; Day
Enrolment	698 girls
Denomination	Roman Catholic
Fees	No

St Mary's CBS

Address	Millpark Road, Enniscorthy, Co. Wexford
Telephone	054-34330
Email	cbs@iol.ie
Principal	John Ryan
School Type	Secondary; Day
Enrolment	575 boys
Denomination	Roman Catholic
Fees	No

Enniscorthy Vocational College

Address	Enniscorthy, Co. Wexford
Telephone	053-34185
Email	evcplc@eircom.net
Principal	Majella Stafford
School Type	Vocational; Day
Enrolment	334 boys; 484 girls
Denomination	Interdenominational
Fees	No

Gorey Community School

Address	Esmonde Street, Gorey, Co. Wexford
Telephone	055-21000
Email	officegcs@iol.ie
Principal	Nicholas Sweetman
School Type	Community; Day
Enrolment	760 boys; 796 girls
Denomination	Interdenominational
Fees	No

Kilmuckridge Vocational College

Address	Kilmuckridge, Gorey, Co. Wexford
Telephone	053-30169
Email	kilmuck.ias@eircom.net
Principal	Seamus Redmond
School Type	Vocational; Day
Enrolment	102 boys; 95 girls
Denomination	Interdenominational
Fees	No

Ramsgrange Community School

Address	Ramsgrange, New Ross, Co. Wexford
Telephone	051-389211
Email	ramsgrange@eircom.net
Principal	Liam Fardy
School Type	Community; Day
Enrolment	220 boys; 213 girls
Denomination	Interdenominational
Fees	No

Christian Brothers Secondary School

Address	Mountgarrett, New Ross, Co. Wexford
Telephone	051-421384
Email	cbsnr.ias@eircom.net
Principal	Raymond Murray
School Type	Secondary; Day
Enrolment	110 boys; 55 girls
Denomination	Roman Catholic
Fees	No

Good Counsel College

Address	New Ross, Co. Wexford
Telephone	051-421182
Email	info@goodcounselcollege.ie
Principal	Fr John Hennebry
School Type	Secondary; Day
Enrolment	711 boys
Denomination	Roman Catholic
Fees	No

Our Lady of Lourdes Secondary School

Address	Rosbercon, New Ross, Co. Wexford
Telephone	051-422177
Email	ourladyoflourdes.ias@eircom.net
Principal	Ken Moroney
School Type	Secondary; Day
Enrolment	302 girls
Denomination	Roman Catholic
Fees	No

New Ross Vocational College

Address	New Ross, Co. Wexford
Telephone	051-421278
Email	office@nrvoccollege.ie
Principal	Pat Murphy
School Type	Vocational; Day
Enrolment	101 boys; 174 girls
Denomination	Interdenominational
Fees	No

St Mary's Secondary School

Address	Irishtown, New Ross, Co. Wexford
Telephone	051-421637
Email	officesecretary@eircom.net
Principal	Gene O'Sullivan
School Type	Secondary; Day
Enrolment	492 girls
Denomination	Roman Catholic
Fees	No

Christian Brothers Secondary School

Address	Thomas Street, Wexford Town
Telephone	053-9141391
Email	admin@wexfordcbs.org
Principal	Frank Duke
School Type	Secondary; Day
Enrolment	434 boys
Denomination	Roman Catholic
Fees	No

Loreto Secondary School

Address	Spawell Road, Wexford Town
Telephone	053-9142783
Email	loretowexford@eircom.net
Principal	Billy O'Shea
School Type	Secondary; Day
Enrolment	654 girls
Denomination	Roman Catholic
Fees	No

Presentation Secondary School

Address	Grogan's Road, Wexford Town
Telephone	053-24133
Email	preswexford.ias@eircom.net
Principal	G. Croke
School Type	Secondary; Day
Enrolment	606 girls
Denomination	Roman Catholic
Fees	No

St Peter's College

Address	Summerhill, Wexford Town
Telephone	053-9142071
Email	pquigley@stpeterscollege.ie
Principal	Patrick Quigley
School Type	Secondary; Day
Enrolment	656 boys
Denomination	Roman Catholic
Fees	No

Wexford Vocational College

Address	Westgate, Wexford, Co. Wexford
Telephone	053-9122753
Email	office@wexfordvocational.com
Principal	Edward O'Reilly
School Type	Vocational; Day
Enrolment	223 boys; 269 girls
Denomination	Interdenominational
Fees	No

Arklow Community College

Address	Coolgreaney Road, Arklow, Co. Wicklow
Telephone	0402-32149
Email	Seamusmurphy14@eircom.net
Principal	Seamus Murphy
School Type	Vocational; Day
Enrolment	199 boys; 161 girls
Denomination	Interdenominational
Fees	No

CO. WICKLOW

St Kevin's CBS

Address	Coolgreaney Road, Arklow, Co. Wicklow
Telephone	0402-32564
Email	office@arklowcbs.iol.ie
Principal	Charles J. Kavanagh
School Type	Secondary; Day
Enrolment	303 boys
Denomination	Roman Catholic
Fees	No

St Mary's College

Address	St Mary's Road, Arklow, Co. Wicklow
Telephone	0402-32419
Email	stmaryscollege@iolfree.ie
Principal	Sr Síor Cosgrove
School Type	Secondary; Day
Enrolment	557 girls
Denomination	Roman Catholic
Fees	No

Scoil Chonglais

Address	Baltinglass, Co. Wicklow
Telephone	059-6481449
Email	scoilchonglais@eircom.net
Principal	David Hallahan
School Type	Vocational; Day
Enrolment	157 boys; 200 girls
Denomination	Interdenominational
Fees	No

Blessington Community College

Address	Naas Road, Blessington, Co. Wicklow
Telephone	045-865170
Email	blessingtoncc@eircom.net
Principal	Frank McGinn
School Type	Vocational; Day
Enrolment	146 boys; 127 girls
Denomination	Interdenominational
Fees	No

Loreto Secondary School

Address	Vevay Road, Bray, Co. Wicklow
Telephone	01-2867481
Email	loretosecondarybray@eircom.net
Principal	Catherine Donagh
School Type	Secondary; Day
Enrolment	857 girls
Denomination	Roman Catholic
Fees	No

Presentation College

Address	Putland Road, Bray, Co. Wicklow
Telephone	01-2867517
Email	info@presbray.com
Principal	Gerry Duffy
School Type	Secondary; Day
Enrolment	651 boys
Denomination	Roman Catholic
Fees	No

St Brendan's College

Address	Woodbrook, Bray, Co. Wicklow
Telephone	01-2822317
Email	st_brendanscollege@eircom.net
Principal	Tony Bellew
School Type	Secondary; Day
Enrolment	370 boys
Denomination	Roman Catholic
Fees	No

St Gerard's

Address	Thornhill Road, Bray, Co. Wicklow	
Telephone	01-2821822	
Email	office@stgerards.net	
Principal	Michael McMullan	
School Type	Secondary; Day & Boarding	
Enrolment	254 boys; 168 girls	
Denomination	Roman Catholic	
Fees	Day Yes	Boarding Yes

St Killian's Community School

Address	Ballywaltrim, Bray, Co. Wicklow
Telephone	01-2828126
Email	michaelsheridan.ias@eircom.net
Principal	Michael Sheridan
School Type	Community; Day
Enrolment	314 boys; 319 girls
Denomination	Interdenominational
Fees	No

St Thomas' Community College

Address	Novara Avenue, Bray, Co. Wicklow
Telephone	01-2866233
Email	enquiries@stthomascc.ie
Principal	Carol Hanney
School Type	Vocational; Day
Enrolment	362 boys; 744 girls
Denomination	Interdenominational
Fees	No

Coláiste Raithin

Address	Bóthar Florence, Bré, Co. Chill Mhantáin
Telephone	01-2760288
Email	raithin1@indigo.ie
Principal	Gearóid Ó Ciaráin
School Type	Vocational; Day; All tuition through Irish
Enrolment	153 boys; 130 girls
Denomination	Interdenominational
Fees	No

Coláiste Bhríde

Address	Carnew, Co. Wicklow
Telephone	053-9426318
Email	cbcarnew@eircom.net
Principal	Linda Dunne
School Type	Vocational; Day
Enrolment	260 boys; 224 girls
Denomination	Interdenominational
Fees	No

Coláiste Chraobh Abhann

Address	Creowen, Kilcoole, Co. Wicklow
Telephone	01-2870198
Email	reception@colaisteca.ie
Principal	Shane Eivers
School Type	Vocational; Day
Enrolment	121 boys; 70 girls
Denomination	Interdenominational
Fees	No

St Kevin's Community College

Address	Dunlavin, Co. Wicklow
Telephone	045-401223
Email	stkevins@eircom.net
Principal	Padraic Ó Luanaigh
School Type	Vocational; Day
Enrolment	201 boys; 191 girls
Denomination	Interdenominational
Fees	No

St David's Secondary Co-Educational School

Address	Greystones, Co. Wicklow
Telephone	01-2874800
Email	davids.ias@tinet.ie
Principal	Jacinta Jones
School Type	Secondary; Day
Enrolment	278 boys; 242 girls
Denomination	Roman Catholic
Fees	No

Avondale Community College

Address	Rathdrum, Co. Wicklow
Telephone	0404-46445
Email	adaleccadmin@tinet.ie
Principal	John Walshe
School Type	Vocational; Day
Enrolment	252 boys; 179 girls
Denomination	Interdenominational
Fees	No

Abbey Community College

Address	Wicklow Town, Co. Wicklow
Telephone	0404-67567
Email	abbeycc.ias@eircom.net
Principal	Thomas Tyrrell
School Type	Vocational; Day
Enrolment	295 boys; 120 girls
Denomination	Interdenominational
Fees	No

De La Salle College

Address	St Mantan's Road, Wicklow Town, Co. Wicklow
Telephone	0404-67581
Email	delasallewicklow@eircom.net
Principal	Michael Dempsey
School Type	Secondary; Day
Enrolment	281 boys
Denomination	Roman Catholic
Fees	No

Dominican College

Address	Wicklow Town, Co. Wicklow
Telephone	0404-68111
Email	info@dcw.ie
Principal	Mary White
School Type	Secondary; Day
Enrolment	515 girls
Denomination	Roman Catholic
Fees	No

East Glendalough School

Address	Station Road, Wicklow Town, Co. Wicklow
Telephone	0404-69608
Email	eastglendalough@eircom.net
Principal	Alan Cox
School Type	Comprehensive; Day
Enrolment	194 boys; 167 girls
Denomination	Church of Ireland
Fees	No